SURRENDER

THE KEY TO ETERNAL LIFE

B.T. SWAMI

HARI NAMA PRESS

Hari-Nama Press gratefully acknowledges the BBT for the use of verses and purports from Śrīla Prabhupāda's books.

First printing 2013
Second edition: Amazon KDP 2020

Layout by Jayānanda dāsa
Cover design by Tamāl Kṛṣṇa dāsa

ISBN: 9798643777687

SURRENDER

THE KEY TO ETERNAL LIFE

Contents

Acknowledgements i

Foreword iii

Editor's Preface ix

Chapter 1: Humility with Determination Guarantees Success 1

The Sparrow's Eggs
Gaining Parole from Illusion
Real Humility Means No Enemies
Envy Increases the False Ego
Tough Love
Workaholism Does Not Signify Advancement

Chapter 2: One Who Is Envious Cannot Advance 19

Envy Exiles Us from Vaikuṇṭha
Śrīla Prabhupāda Encounters Envy
Envy Prevents Us from Following Scripture
Envy Amongst Vaiṣṇavas
Relating to Juniors
Relating to Equals
Envy Means Violence
Introspection Is Vital

Chapter 3: Loving Our Neighbors More Than Ourselves 37

The Necessary Preparation
Breaking Free of Materialism
Compassion Is the Key
Entering the Anti-Material Realm
Truly Feeling for Others
Gratitude Increases Compassion
Depth of Compassion Indicates Advancement
Selfishness Keeps Us Imprisoned
Selflessness Empowers Us Unlimitedly

Chapter 4: The Language of Selflessness 63

Understanding Śrīla Prabhupāda's Instruction
Are We Truly Selfless?
Learning the Language of Selflessness

Taking Care of the Real Number One
Anxiety and Low Self-Esteem Block Selflessness
Why Am I Bored?
Dissatisfaction Indicates Selfishness
We Are Only Caretakers
Selflessness Means Divine Strength
Being Brave

CHAPTER 5: When We Wound the Spiritual Master 83

Refusal to Surrender Blocks the Paramparā
Spiritual versus Material Weaponry
Ambiguity Is Māyā
Anti-Material Strategies
ISKCON Comes from the Spiritual World
Lightening the Burden of the Spiritual Master

CHAPTER 6: Dedicate This Life to the Lord 101

Finding True Love
Material Time versus Transcendental Time
Real Friends
Spiritualizing Sleep
Expect Miracles

CHAPTER 7: Losing Oneself to Gain Oneself 129

Addressing Inner and Institutional Conflict
Mundane Morality Is Not Enough
Why Many Spiritualists Fail
Losing Oneself to Gain Oneself
How to Continue Year after Year
Today I Died
What Is My Status?
Why I Write
Fear of Killing the False Ego
Withholding Love Means Cheating Ourselves
The Dangers of Not Loving
Have No Enemies
Lord Jesus' Enormous Love for Judas
Reassessing after Years in the Movement

ABOUT THE AUTHOR 159

Acknowledgements

Hari-Nama Press would like to sincerely thank Deborah Klein and Līlā-Kathā devī dāsī for their extensive editing work. We would also like to thank Jayānanda dāsa for proofreading and layout, and for performing any task necessary to get this book to print. We are grateful to Puruṣa-sūkta dāsa for ensuring the philosophical accuracy of the material, and to Kripa devī dāsī for proofreading. The Press would also like to thank the BBT for providing the cover image, and Tamāl Kṛṣṇa dāsa for designing the cover and front matter. Finally, we would like to thank all of the individuals who spent many hours transcribing the material for this book. Hari-Nama Press is fortunate to have a great team of individuals who remain dedicated to publishing the words of Bhakti Tirtha Swami.

Foreword

Śrīmad-Bhāgavatam, a sacred text compiled five thousand years ago, makes a bold prediction:

> *tad-vāg-visargo janatāgha-viplavo*
> *yasmin prati-ślokam abaddhavaty api*
> *nāmāny anantasya yaśo 'ṅkitāni yac*
> *chṛṇvanti gāyanti gṛṇanti sādhavaḥ*

> [T]hat literature which is full of descriptions of the transcendental glories of the name, fame, forms, pastimes, etc., of the unlimited Supreme Lord is a different creation, full of transcendental words directed toward bringing about a revolution in the impious lives of this world's misdirected civilization. Such transcendental literatures, even though imperfectly composed, are heard, sung, and accepted by purified men who are thoroughly honest.*

At the time that the *Bhāgavatam* was recorded, the entire world was ruled by Vedic kings who supported the divine culture; the civilization was not "misdirected." Only later, with the gradual vitiation of Vedic culture, did the world's civilization become misguided, and so the above verse anticipates a revolution to be effected by the presentation and distribution of *Śrīmad-Bhāgavatam*, which of all Vedic texts most fully describes the transcendental names, forms, qualities, pastimes, and associates of the Supreme Personality of Godhead.

---

* *Śrīmad-Bhāgavatam* 1.5.11

The person who fulfilled the prediction is Śrī Śrīmad A.C. Bhaktivedanta Swami Prabhupāda—he translated *Śrīmad-Bhāgavatam* from Sanskrit into English, with comprehensive purports, and inspired its translation into fifty languages and its profuse distribution in countries throughout the world.

In the course of his efforts, Śrīla Prabhupāda attracted many young men and women who embraced the principles of *Śrīmad-Bhāgavatam* and the *Bhagavad-gītā*, adopted the practices of Kṛṣṇa (God) consciousness, *bhakti-yoga*, and endeavored to distribute the divine message for the benefit of all living beings.

One such spiritual revolutionary was Bhakti Tīrtha Swami. During Śrīla Prabhupāda's lifetime, Bhakti Tīrtha Swami excelled in distributing *Śrīmad-Bhāgavatam* and other sacred texts presented by Śrīla Prabhupāda, including to scholars in the communist countries behind the Iron Curtain. Later, he pioneered the mission in several African nations and in many African American communities. He was, as Śrīla Prabhupāda instructed him to be, "selfless, humble, and brave."

Śrīla Prabhupāda understood *Śrīmad-Bhāgavatam* as a universal principle, or science, that transcends sectarian designations and considerations. When a woman asked him "Is there anyone similar to Joan of Arc in the *Śrīmad-Bhāgavatam*?" he replied, "You want to see Joan of Arc in *Śrīmad-Bhāgavatam*? Why don't you take Joan of Arc of *Śrīmad-Bhāgavatam*?" He explained that *bhāgavatam*, or *bhāgavata*, comes from the Sanskrit word Bhagavān, which means God, and refers to anything pertaining to God. Thus anything in relation to God, "any activities of devotees—that is *Śrīmad-Bhāgavatam*." So if Joan of Arc was in relationship with God, she is also *Bhāgavatam*. And so *Bhāgavatam* can be expanded without limit.

Surrender: The Key to Eternal Life is an expansion of *Śrīmad-Bhāgavatam*—a continuation of the spiritual revolution. In this book Bhakti Tīrtha Swami presents the same teachings as the original *Bhāgavatam*, but with his own experiences and realizations, and in his own words, perfectly suitable for his audience. It is all about God and those in relationship with God, those who want to work for His cause—and about those who work against it.

In *Surrender*, Bhakti Tīrtha Swami appeals to us to become spiritual warriors and fight the forces of ignorance and destructiveness in the world, in communities, and even within ourselves—and he gives us the required weapons, or tools, to do so.

How to read *Śrīmad-Bhāgavatam* or *Bhagavad gītā*, and by extension *Surrender*, is explained by Bhakti Tīrtha Swami in the book itself:

> *When we read* Bhagavad-gītā, Śrīmad-Bhāgavatam, *and* Rāmāyaṇa, *we should clearly understand that these scriptures are just as alive as we are. Never read the scriptures as if they are simply a collection of stories. We should not approach any type of holy book merely to derive data from it, but rather in a mood of appreciating it as a living, literary incarnation of God. To the extent that we engage with the scriptures in an appreciative, personal mood, to that extent will they take on a live quality for us. . . . By approaching our literature with great devotion and care, we can eventually gain admittance to the very pastimes about which we now read.*

Of all the enemies of our true self-interest, which is to realize God and our eternal loving relationship with Him, the most formidable are the enemies within, our own internal weaknesses. And Bhakti Tīrtha Swami, the great spiritual warrior, leads us in that effort as well. With great humility and candor, he encourages us by his own example:

I am often asked variations of the following questions: "How do you continue year after year in your spiritual life? How do you avoid being disturbed by so many conflicts, institutional turmoil, and planetary instability?" To be honest, I am disturbed. Spiritual life is not easy for me. I find every day a challenge. Yet, I have managed to remain within the process due to the mercy of my spiritual master. I practice introspection rigorously. It is healthy to question ourselves periodically, to inquire internally, "To what degree have I become a distinct part of spiritual culture? To what degree does my particular tradition remain a theory upon which I ponder, but in which I do not fully believe? To what degree do I embrace our philosophy within my heart?" Everyone in the conditioned state is undergoing difficulties. At the same time, Kṛṣṇa assists each one and has no favorites. Although we may have different levels of sukṛti, *or devotional credits, according to our past lives, each must pass tests designed by the Lord to perfectly fit his or her capacity.*

A surefire way to remain fixed in devotional life is to perform constant inventory of our progress and commitment. I personally undertake monthly inventory, yearly inventory, and even inventory by decades. I also closely examine the behavior of those who are advancing steadily. I ask myself, "What are they doing that I am not? What is working for them?" As spiritualists, we should expect to personally have the experiences of transcendence promised by our individual traditions. Each one of us can absorb ourselves more and more in God consciousness. Unequivocally, some people on this planet will become God conscious in this lifetime. Let us aim to include ourselves in that quota. It is possible.

And he assures us that the scriptures and saints—which to my mind include Bhakti Tīrtha Swami himself, and this book—will help us all the way:

> *[W]hen we really make God our top priority, miracles unfold. Realizing that we have to do our part, we trust that the mercy of the Lord's servants is always accessible. This mood of simultaneous endeavor and surrender allows us to move quickly in our devotional service... By making the scriptures our life experience, by appreciating the great saints in various traditions (what to speak of those in the Vaiṣṇava line), and by realizing that they are there for us, we will attain their shelter and their love without delay.*

I am confident that anyone who reads *Surrender* in this mood and earnestly applies it in his or her life will achieve the loving shelter of Śrīpāda Bhakti Tīrtha Swami, Śrīla Prabhupāda, their spiritual predecessors, and ultimately the Divine Couple in the spiritual kingdom of God, and live with them eternally.

Hare Kṛṣṇa.

Girirāja Swami
September 27, 2012
Śrīla Bhaktivinoda Ṭhākura's Appearance Day
Dallas

Editor's Preface

Many readers familiar with the life of Bhakti Tīrtha Swami may wonder how Hari-Nama Press has published a new book, considering that he left this world on June 27, 2005. Printing an author's book posthumously warrants an explanation.

In 2004, after Mahārāja had received his diagnosis of cancer, he continued working on his books with the same intensity as always. In a letter to the editors dated January 5, 2005, he wrote, "Now that my time in this body seems to be rather limited, let's see how many books we can get out before my departure." Between 2004 and 2005, he wrote another book in the Beggar series, *The Beggar IV: Die Before Dying*, which we were able to print before he left this world. Not only was he focused on writing his Beggar prayers, which he completed during his rigorous cancer treatments, but his gaze was fixed on the future of his books as well as on the future of Hari-Nama Press. He held many meetings that year with the team during which he shared his desires for the continuation of the Press in his absence. More specifically, he worked with the editors to organize several books for future publication, ensuring that the Hari-Nama Press team would be engaged in service well after his departure.

At the beginning of 2005, Bhakti Tīrtha Swami requested his book team to begin work on this current volume, which he entitled *Surrender: The Key to Eternal Life*. Deborah Klein completed the initial editing of the book and then sent the manuscript to Līlā Kaṭha dāsī to prepare the final draft. After Mahārāja left this world, however, we were engaged in publishing several reprints of his other works, which were rapidly selling out. Due to the great demand for his writings, the editing of *Surrender* had to be delayed. Fortunately, we are now able to offer this new volume of transcendental wisdom. Since Mahārāja authorized us to print several books after his departure, we expect that this will not be his final publication—no doubt to the relief and pleasure of his many readers and well-wishers!

Surrender: The Key to Eternal Life is a deep meditation on topics such as the cultivation of humility and selflessness, as well as on the detrimental effects of envy, anxiety, and boredom. As usual, Bhakti Tīrtha Swami's work contains specific and practical ways to engage in spiritual life. Mahārāja wants us to look at our weaknesses. Instead of leaving us to wallow in the muck of our *anarthas*, he encourages us to take inventory of them so that we can make genuine changes and advancement. He was especially compassionate in his approach to *anartha-nivṛtti*, understanding that many of us have a hard time relinquishing bad habits that we have carried with us lifetime after lifetime, even while trying sincerely to chant and hear the Lord's holy name. Through his compassion, he listened to devotees, asked questions, and took care to pinpoint the exact nature of the problems that often trouble the individual and the community of devotees. He would address such concerns in person, in his lectures, and in his books.

Reading *Surrender*, you will experience the palpable presence of Bhakti Tīrtha Swami as he continues to push us forward, encouraging us to look at ourselves so that we can reach deeper levels of devotional experience and practice. It can be frightening to introspect with such brutal honesty, and indeed, it takes great courage. For this reason, Mahārāja consistently uses the term "spiritual warrior." It takes strength and valor to battle the mind and senses, but it is a battle that we do not have to face alone. Bhakti Tīrtha Swami, a true spiritual warrior, is present and available to us throughout these pages, encouraging us and coaching us as we read. His spirit will no doubt guide us as we apply this wisdom to our lives.

During those last few months, Mahārāja frequently told us that everything he needed to say was in his books. Nothing remained that was not written down or spoken in his lectures. On behalf of the entire Hari-Nama Press team, we are very grateful to present this book to the Vaiṣṇava community and continue the legacy of Bhakti Tīrtha Mahārāja. We hope his words of inspiration, lovingly collected in the following pages, will help you in your spiritual lives as much as it has helped us in ours. Hare Kṛṣṇa!

CHAPTER 1

Humility with Determination Guarantees Success

The Sparrow's Eggs

In *Caitanya-caritāmṛta, Madhya-līlā* 19.151, Lord Śrī Caitanya Mahāprabhu instructs Śrīla Rūpa Gosvāmī in Prayāga with the following words:

brahmāṇḍa bhramite kona bhāgyavān jīva
guru-kṛṣṇa-prasāde pāya bhakti-latā-bīja

> The living entity wanders throughout different planets in different forms and bodies, but if by chance he comes in contact with a bona fide spiritual master, by the grace of the spiritual master he receives Lord Kṛṣṇa's shelter, and his devotional life begins.

Once a living entity finally comes in contact with *sādhu* (a saintly person), *guru* (the spiritual master), and the Supreme Lord, much of his or her progress depends upon how determined he or she is to attain transcendental goals. Perseverance and determination are amongst the most significant factors in developing our Kṛṣṇa consciousness.

By focusing on important goals, the *jīva* develops more clarity, realization, and perseverance. Certain situations which occur within our Kṛṣṇa conscious communities and practices may seem insurmountable to us. However, humility combined with determination can lead to results beyond what we think possible. In his purport to *Bhagavad-gītā* 6.24, Śrīla Prabhupāda narrates the following story:

> *A sparrow laid her eggs on the shore of the ocean, but the big ocean carried away the eggs on its waves. The sparrow became very upset and asked the ocean to return her eggs. The ocean did not even consider her appeal. So the sparrow decided to dry up the ocean. She began to pick out the water in her small beak, and everyone laughed at her for her impossible determination. The news of her activity spread, and at last Garuḍa, the gigantic bird carrier of Lord Viṣṇu, heard it. He became compassionate toward his small sister bird, and so he came to see the sparrow. Garuḍa was very pleased by the determination of the small sparrow, and he promised to help. Thus Garuḍa at once asked the ocean to return her eggs lest he himself take up the work of the sparrow. The ocean was frightened at this, and returned the eggs. Thus the sparrow became happy by the grace of Garuḍa.*
>
> *Similarly, the practice of* yoga, *especially* bhakti-yoga *in Kṛṣṇa consciousness, may appear to be a very difficult job. But if anyone follows the principles with great determination, the Lord will surely help, for God helps those who help themselves.*

What is most significant about the story Śrīla Prabhupāda narrates is that the little sparrow demonstrated such determination despite amazing odds stacked against her. Consequently, a tiny bird succeeded in forcing the great ocean to surrender. Similarly, so much of our development and growth in Kali-yuga, in this current age of hypocrisy and quarrel, is based on doing the right thing in the face of seemingly insurmountable obstacles posed by our minds, senses, and environment. In spite of these difficulties, however, if we act properly, Kṛṣṇa will then come to our aid. In *Bhagavad-gītā* 10.10, Kṛṣṇa promises:

teṣāṁ satata-yuktānāṁ
bhajatāṁ prīti-pūrvakam
dadāmi buddhi-yogaṁ taṁ
yena mām upayānti te

> To those who are constantly devoted to serving Me with love, I give the understanding by which they can come to Me.

Kṛṣṇa's statement is very powerful. He declares unequivocally that He will intervene on our behalf if we exhibit steadiness and determination. The sages at Naimiṣāraṇya, for instance, were determined to remain in the forest for as long as necessary to understand the truth even if they had to leave their bodies. They had come from so many places, from so many backgrounds, with so many different understandings, but they were not content because they had not yet heard about developing pure devotional service. Śrīmad-Bhāgavatam 1.2.6 describes that the sages, determined to discover the highest activity for everyone in this age of Kali, prayed until Sūta Gosvāmī appeared and explained to them:

sa vai puṁsāṁ paro dharmo
yato bhaktir adhokṣaje
ahaituky apratihatā
yayātmā suprasīdati

> The supreme occupation [*dharma*] for all humanity is that by which men can attain to loving devotional service unto the transcendent Lord. Such devotional service must be unmotivated and uninterrupted to completely satisfy the self.

The highest activities are those that will help us attain unmotivated, loving service to Kṛṣṇa. The sages did not hear that the best path in life is *haṭha-yoga*, *jñāna-yoga*, *kriyā-yoga*, *aṣṭāṅga-yoga*, *rāja-yoga*, *kuṇḍalinī-yoga*, religion, rituals, or fruitive activities. No. Instead, they discovered that attaining the highest goal involves undertaking a shift in consciousness, humbling oneself to such an extent that nothing is left but purity. Where humility is lacking, impurities creep in and contaminate everything. Keep in mind that we are in the material world and the material body because we are cheaters and deviants. We are sinful and very prone to what the human body is designed for: making mistakes and being in illusion. Serious devotees desire the vision to see the illusions they have created in order to dissolve them. If we adopt the mindset of wondering who can help us deal with our illusions, where we can go, what we can do, then we will constantly grow. Discovering ourselves to be imprisoned, we should accept that we have committed crimes against God and need to be rehabilitated.

Gaining Parole from Illusion

One of the quickest ways to gain parole is to combine humility with determination in devotional service. When we lack humility, we develop the tendency to focus on someone else's faults rather than our own. When others try to show us our faults, we immediately see their observations as stemming from their own imperfections, and not our own. Therefore, we conclude that we are okay—but we are not okay because nobody in a material body is okay. If we fully understood our faults, then we would not be in the material world in the first place. Kṛṣṇa, in the heart and through *sādhu, śāstra* (sacred scriptures), and *guru*, constantly shows us what it is we need to adjust in ourselves. Humility is so significant that its presence or absence indicates perfectly the degree of a devotee's advancement. One who constantly looks within to see what has to be eliminated will quickly advance. Elimination is essential because we are already eternally connected with Kṛṣṇa. We are pure, but this purity is covered over. Our spiritual life basically involves uncovering. It is that simple and that difficult. When our faults are revealed, what do we do? Some people who are sleeping become angry when you wake them up. They want to be left alone.

For this reason, when Kṛṣṇa comes, most people do not know His real identity. They miss out because they do not want to accept that they are prisoners in a world of illusion. The crazier a person is, the more she views everyone else as insane rather than herself. An insane person might roam the streets without proper clothes and eat out of garbage cans, while at the same time thinking how ridiculous other people are. She may even imagine she is happy. After all, she can sleep anywhere, while other people have to work, take baths, and change clothes. A person with mental illness might assume that nothing is wrong with him, even though he may wear five coats in the middle of summer. Imagining that others are envious, he dismisses them when they look at him askance, and tell him to take off his coats. Mentally disturbed people frequently cannot change their situations. Assuming themselves to be completely sane, they refuse to hear from others.

While those with grave mental incoherence will rarely ask for help, regular people usually turn to others when they experience problems. They may even see a doctor or a therapist. While ordinary people are aware when something in their lives is awry, those who are certified insane will not only refuse to ask for help, but will resist receiving assistance if it is offered. Those who seek help frequently recover as a result of their efforts. But extremely ill people sometimes have to be confined or strapped down before they are able to receive medical care. Oblivious to reality, they must be separated from the general public during their engagement with illusion. While fortunate, in one sense, that we can function in the external world, we should realize that the material world itself is one big mental hospital in which living entities are absorbed in the illusion that their suffering is pleasurable.

For instance, when Lord Indra was cursed by his spiritual master, Bṛhaspati, to become a pig, he initially thought of his situation as abominable. But by the time Lord Brahmā descended to invite him to ascend once again to his position as King of Heaven, Indra refused. Indra now perceived Lord Brahmā's invitation as a disturbance to his sense gratification. "I have come to remind you about what you have forgotten," Śrīla Prabhupāda would sometimes tell the public. Sometimes it is painful to be reminded. Śrīla Prabhupāda's direct approach would disturb some people. The deeper their illusion, the more anger they would feel when they heard the truth. Of all the elements defined in *Bhagavad-gītā*

7.4 which confine us to this material prison—earth, water, fire, air, ether, mind, intelligence, and false ego—the false ego is the most pervasive. The false ego was one of the first elements Lord Brahmā created when he manifested the material universe. He created the misconception of bodily identification, which the *Vedas* call *ahaṅkāra*. The prison environment revolves around false ego, which is impossible to dissolve without transcendental assistance.

Real Humility Means No Enemies

A practical way to calculate our personal level of humility is to notice the extent to which we maintain the mindset of friends and enemies. Kṛṣṇa has said that one who is dear to Him has neither enemies nor friends. Even if someone acts as our enemy, we do not have to view them as such. Not having enemies does not mean that we are in denial, or that we avoid addressing improper behavior. We address issues out of love and with humility by speaking truthfully. At the same time, we should try not to see others as enemies, whether they agree with us or not.

The most exemplary humility was displayed by Lord Caitanya during his interactions with Rāmacandra Purī. Rāmacandra Purī, an extremely envious and devious godbrother of Mahāprabhu's *guru*, Īśvara Purī, challenged Lord Caitanya by pointing out the Lord's seemingly improper behavior. Spotting ants in Mahāprabhu's room, Rāmacandra Purī immediately came to the conclusion that Mahāprabhu was indulging in sweets and thus not controlling His senses. Did Lord Caitanya respond by arguing, or criticizing Rāmacandra Purī as well? No, not only did Lord Caitanya refuse to defend Himself, but He immediately changed his daily habits by eating only half as usual, even though He was the Supreme Lord.

Subsequently, Rāmacandra Purī challenged Lord Caitanya further by claiming that His altered conduct signified artificial renunciation. Did Lord Caitanya protest at this point? Initially, He was told that He eats too much, and then He was told that He eats too little. Instead of highlighting this contradiction, the Lord demonstrates the position of real strength by humbly accepting the criticism of His *guru's* godbrother. A person who possesses true spiritual strength feels genuinely humbled in the face of criticism, even if it may be unjust. He or she constantly meditates, "I want to know Kṛṣṇa more, I want to serve Kṛṣṇa more; therefore, Kṛṣṇa is helping me in so many unexpected ways." An authentic devotee constantly looks for ways to be freed of the illusion.

A devotee feels very subservient, always thinking that he or she is the worst servant of all. We see this example in the writings of the *ācāryas* in our disciplic succession. An *ācārya* is a spiritual master who teaches by his own example. Genuinely imagining that no one is more fallen than they are, they fervently pray for help. The neophyte devotee, however, refuses to accept feedback and sometimes even tries to blaspheme those who attempt to help him see his own suffering. Even if we feel that we are right and the other person is just trying to put us down, then we have even more of a reason to be humble. By helping those who criticize to understand what is proper by showing humility, we let *bhakti*, or pure devotional service, prevail.

Lord Caitanya did just that when Rāmacandra Purī attacked Him. *Śāstra* tells us that Rāmacandra did not have the Lord's best interest in mind; he was merely faultfinding. Nevertheless, Lord Caitanya accepted his so-called instructions and made a shift in His own behavior. A person who has great strength does not get swayed by popular sentiment, by fads, by friends or enemies. Rather, he or she is always blissful. When a devotee meditates that Kṛṣṇa is everywhere, including in her own heart, then she will naturally wonder why she has not returned to Him yet. Deeply aware that Kṛṣṇa is calling us constantly, we want to know what is blocking our progress. We must take the humble position and desperately search after what is obfuscating our return home. Let us be eager to perceive whatever weaknesses we have, with the realization that these flaws are responsible for our position in this material world.

Envy Increases the False Ego

It is also possible to evaluate our current state of humility by watching our minds in different situations. If one of our peers is glorified in our presence, observe the degree to which our minds become envious. If we feel intense negativity, we can understand that we have a deep level of contamination. We should recognize that this is the reason that we are in the material world in the first place. Attaining liberation means becoming non-envious and not seeing ourselves as the proprietors. We all possess an envious mentality. If we maintain it, we will stay at the same level of consciousness year after year. How powerful it would be if instead of protesting, we humbly accept and simply apply the advice of those who might not have the best of intentions! If we cannot do that, then we are undoubtedly still disqualified from attaining Goloka Vṛndāvana, our eternal home. Experiencing enviousness means that our creeper is still very much in the neophyte stage. Kṛṣṇa clarifies this point in *Bhagavad-gītā* 12.13-14:

adveṣṭā sarva-bhūtānāṁ
maitraḥ karuṇa eva ca
nirmamo nirahaṅkāraḥ
sama-duḥkha-sukhaḥ kṣamī

santuṣṭaḥ satataṁ yogī
yatātmā dṛḍha-niścayaḥ
mayy arpita-mano-buddhir
yo mad-bhaktaḥ sa me priyaḥ

> One who is not envious but is a kind friend to all living entities, who does not think himself a proprietor and is free from false ego, who is equal in both happiness and distress, who is tolerant, always satisfied, self-controlled, and engaged in devotional service with determination, his mind and intelligence fixed on Me—such a devotee of Mine is very dear to Me.

When we hear that the other devotees on our team distributed more books than us, what is our mood? Do we feel happy that one of our peers did so well, or do we become frustrated that he or she won again? We must look closely at what is going through our minds. If we encounter many negative thoughts, then we should realize that we have a problem. We want to think of others without enviousness, and support them in their service to *guru* and Kṛṣṇa. We should glorify their good qualities, and try to emulate them. We should ask others for their blessings. The mind is very powerful and can play so many unusual games. However, if we can have the determination of the sparrow and work with a similar perseverance, then Kṛṣṇa or His devotees will come to our aid. The more Kṛṣṇa sees that we actually want to come to Him, the more He will provide. If we choose not to come to Him, we can put so many other things in His place. We will miss out when we decide to hold on to our *ahaṅkāra*, or false ego.

Observe how the *ahaṅkāra* surfaces in amazing ways, even among intimate friends or family members. For instance, two women can be the best of friends. Others may even consider them to be inseparable. But when one of them has a baby and the other does not, enviousness may arise between them and poison their relationship. Similarly, when one colleague gets a raise at work and the other does not, their entire interaction may become hostile even though formerly they were on good terms with each other. Such is the power of envy. Sometimes a mother may be envious of her own daughter or a father of his son. As her daughter matures into a young beauty, a mother may feel jealous because she is getting older. A father may see his son developing a business more successful than his own, and he, too, may grow angry. Envy has the power to incite viciousness and division amongst those closest to us. We have to be extremely careful.

Why is Kṛṣṇa giving Arjuna so much information and guidance? Arjuna is *anasūya*, uncontaminated by envy. Because Arjuna is a true friend of Kṛṣṇa, he is able to hear the Lord's confidential transmission and understand His message. In *Bhagavad-gītā* 10.1, the Lord promises to give Arjuna further enlightenment because he values Arjuna's friendship. When one is *anasūya*, then one is able to appreciate the truth at a deeper level. Envy, however, blocks the transmission. It is an emotion which seriously obfuscates a person's vision, greatly reducing his ability to become enthusiastically fixed on the devotional path. Often, we do not even realize the degree to which envy of our peers contaminates our relationships.

Envy is a byproduct of the false ego. We have to look at ourselves and ask whether we are happy with our progress in devotional life. If so, we should continue with what we are doing. Ultimately, however, which intelligent person is happy? Which intelligent devotee is happy? The devotee always wants to become more surrendered. Even if one is freed from the modes of material nature, one still feels sadness regarding others stuck in the material energy. On Brahmaloka, for instance, the residents do not suffer due to their own misfortune, but rather feel distressed that other living entities in the universe are deprived of true happiness. Of course, these fortunate souls live for a long time and experience many pleasures, but ultimately, they also must die.

A new devotee recently approached me with concern because he could not help but notice that many senior devotees around the world have lost their devotion. New devotees observe this phenomenon with fear. Actually, it should frighten us. We should wonder how such a phenomenon occurs and find ways to avoid the same result. A devotee always thinks of how to both sympathize and practically assist another to come back into the fire of devotional service. Ego causes a person to think that such a situation will never happen to him because he sees himself as different. While others may fall down, he sees himself as strong. In his mind, he is virtually immune to such consequences. However, the same Māyā-devī, or the personification of the Lord's illusory energy, is always present. She has many varieties of tricks to bring people down in different ways. In most cases, a person who becomes captured by Māyā-devī did not realize that he or she was in *māyā*, or illusion, until it was too late. Many times, devotees are in *māyā*, but think that they are fine until they undergo such devastation that it becomes impossible not to see the reality of their position.

Tough Love

If we do not have humility, we will simply be a disturbance. Kṛṣṇa will give us so much assistance, but if He sees that we are not taking it, He will help us through tough love, just as a parent should help a child. Sometimes a parent loves a child by embracing her or speaking sweet words to her, but when the child stubbornly ignores her mother or father's guidance, a loving parent chastises her and devises a particular schedule for her rectification. That chastisement is also love. The parent's concern is to help the stubborn child distinguish between what is proper and what is improper.

We have been so determined to be separate from Kṛṣṇa that we have remained in this material universe for millions of lifetimes. Can we not apply similar determination in attaining our release? Lord Kṛṣṇa advises us in *Bhagavad-gītā* 9.22:

ananyāś cintayanto māṁ
ye janāḥ paryupāsate
teṣāṁ nityābhiyuktānāṁ
yoga-kṣemaṁ vahāmy aham

> But those who always worship Me with exclusive devotion, meditating on My transcendental form—to them I carry what they lack, and I preserve what they have.

In this way, a devotee always thinks big. A devotee realizes that Kṛṣṇa accommodates our desires. In other ages, we would be held accountable for even having a sinful thought, but Kali-yuga is different. Rather, just by thinking devotionally, we will get reciprocation based on the mind, the intelligence, and the body. As we try to arrange an offering for the Lord, we should remember that the ultimate result is not even ours anyway. Kṛṣṇa can let it happen or not, but if we humble ourselves enough, Kṛṣṇa will empower us to serve when we make the endeavor. The service attitude is much more important than the service rendered. Sometimes people think that spiritual life is about following all the rituals nicely. Not really. We are engaged in *sādhana-bhakti*, or devotional service according to specific rules and regulations, as a means to develop genuine Kṛṣṇa consciousness.

Workaholism Does Not Signify Advancement

Sometimes we think we are wonderful because we are doing service for Kṛṣṇa and *guru*. We must remember, however, that we are not workaholics, even though we work as hard as we can. We endeavor intensely, but simultaneously strive to develop an abundance of devotion. If we do not cultivate the proper devotional consciousness, we can continue chanting for many lifetimes and still not reach the goal. Ultimately, everything we do as devotees is to assist in the development of proper consciousness.

Notice how Śrīla Prabhupāda called this society the International Society for Kṛṣṇa Consciousness. We do all kinds of work and are often overworked because serious devotees want to do so many things for *guru* and Kṛṣṇa, but are *guru* and Kṛṣṇa flattered by the work? If Kṛṣṇa only wanted the work, then why do we notice that seasoned devotees sometimes fall away from the path? After all, many of these older devotees have done so much work. If it were just a matter of work, they would not fall into *māyā*. Kṛṣṇa would protect them. Work is necessary, but consciousness is more important. If Kṛṣṇa just wanted us to flatter Him and do work for Him, then whoever flatters Him the most, puts in the most hours, and gives the most wealth would be the most advanced. But instead, advancement is measured by the degree to which we are devoid of false ego.

Once we are void of all these *anarthas*, or undesirable personal qualities and attachments, what is left? Our pure state. When someone says something to us or about us, we should think that we are many times worse—and mean it.

Whatever Kṛṣṇa is doing for us, we should think that we are not worthy of it. Kṛṣṇa always arranges facilities for us far beyond our merit and qualification. We can make serious advancement when we put ego on the side. However, any time we find scapegoats or adopt the mentality that everyone is crazy but ourselves, we render ourselves ineligible for parole. Śrīla Prabhupāda explained that in the material world, nearly everyone is crazy. Crazy people feel that they are not accountable to anyone, and frequently commit abominable actions. A few souls will break out of the material world, but most people remain incarcerated.

In summary, we recounted the story of the sparrow who threatened to drink up the ocean in order to emphasize the importance of determination in devotional service. Devotees may easily see themselves as the sparrow. Yes, many forces stand against us, but if we endeavor with pinpointed determination, then Kṛṣṇa will come to facilitate us. This He has already promised.

Question: Is it true that we are somehow responsible whenever a devotee leaves Śrīla Prabhupāda's house?

Answer: It is always true. Śrīla Prabhupāda says that we are to be the caretakers of one another. If we care about others, we want the best for them. Therefore, naturally we feel saddened when those who have come to Śrīla Prabhupāda's movement cannot experience that which is best for them. At the same time, nobody can cause someone else to fall into *māyā* if he or she does not want to. In other words, we can face all kinds of problems, including social, economic, and interpersonal ones, but if a person decides to stop chanting their rounds and to give up following the four rules and regulations, then he or she is responsible for having made that choice. People can lie about us and create all types of problems for us, but nobody can stop us from practicing our Kṛṣṇa consciousness. We stop trying only because we are weak and do not have sufficient faith in Kṛṣṇa.

At the same time, we need to understand that we are all affected by association. The quality of our association can make the process easier by helping us to become more fixed. Conversely, improper association can lead to many difficulties. Many of those who left might well have been able to remain not only within the process of devotional service but also in good standing if the environment had been more supportive. A very strong person will remain fixed regardless of the external situation. The quality of her environment is not important because she wants Kṛṣṇa and is ready to pay whatever price is necessary. However, most people will not possess such pinpointed focus initially. In cases where there is not sufficient facility and encouragement, the majority of people will lose their enthusiasm and fall into *māyā*.

Sometimes after a devotee has fallen back into the material pool, he may want to come back but because nobody calls him or tries to encourage him, he remains distant, too embarrassed to return. Due to the guilt fallen devotees feel about what they did in the past, they often find it difficult to step forward and come back into the association of devotees. They realize that they were mistaken, but the ego is still so strong that it can prevent them from taking that first step. They will sadly remain on the fringe if they are not met with compassion by significant members of the community.

Question: How can we measure our advancement?

Answer: If we find we are envious and the ego still dominates as before, then we should know we are not advancing very much. At the same time, sometimes we are advancing, but still remain in a struggling position. We can distinctly see that we are advancing when we feel more love for Vaiṣṇavas, when we are ready to hear about our faults and act upon them, when we are eager to address our weaknesses, and when we develop increasing determination to become Kṛṣṇa conscious even though presently we may not be very steady.

If our determination is strong and we intensely desire to serve Kṛṣṇa, then we are definitely advancing even if saintly qualities or favorable circumstances have not manifested in our lives yet. It is up to Kṛṣṇa how fast He begins to change the external environment for us or allows certain qualities to become evident. When our desire remains the same or even weaker, then we know we are at risk. The closer we come to Kṛṣṇa, the more we see ourselves as unworthy and fallen. This apparent contradiction is a significant way to measure advancement. When the great *ācāryas* speak about feeling useless and fallen, they are not simply evoking a poetic convention. Since they are so close to Kṛṣṇa and continually experience His love and kindness, they genuinely feel unworthy of what they are receiving. Their humility is sincere and acutely felt.

Those who have not cultivated very much humility will inevitably think highly of themselves, even when they have little to offer. Attributes such as memory, beauty, bodily size, and piety gradually decrease from Satya-yuga, the bygone age of godliness and opulence, to Kali-yuga, our current degraded age. Only one element increases in Kali-yuga—the false ego. Under its spell, the more people lack particular attributes and assets, the more they think they possess. This is the nature of false ego. The more spiritual we are, the less false ego we have, and the more fallen and unworthy we feel. In Kali-yuga, considering ourselves wonderful and expert is a sign of our fallen state. At the same time, we should not immerse ourselves in self-pity, which is another symptom of playing God. Self-pity means that instead of becoming truly humble, we expend our energy feeling sorry for ourselves. Everything still revolves around us. Usually, we are sorry that we do not possess a better body or position which would bring us distinction and adoration. Authentic spiritual sentiments mean feeling genuinely unworthy of having Kṛṣṇa. We must access these sentiments with growing sincerity.

Sometimes we find that particular environments cause us to think too much about sense gratification, weakening our desire to serve and preach. In such cases, we may need a change of environment. Usually, however, a change of environment will not help much because we carry the same mindset with us. What is most important is advanced association. Serious association pulls us forward and pushes us up. It helps us to focus properly on the goal of life and to progress steadily towards it. If we do not have such association, generally we will try, but not really push ourselves very much. Because we are so conditioned to see ourselves as the center of the universe, doing whatever we want, when we want, and how we want, we will usually not find it easy to change.

So much of our devotional life is based on association. When we have good association, we feel more enthusiastic, hear more of the scripture, and seek friendships with those who are trying to live devotionally. If we are feeling low, we may find that we are not taking advantage of good association, or that we are not becoming the higher association we desire. Ultimately, we want to become that higher association. By consistently reinforcing ourselves in Kṛṣṇa consciousness, we will advance quickly and truly become the servant of the servant.

Chapter 2

One Who Is Envious Cannot Advance

Envy Exiles Us from Vaikuṇṭha

Throughout his purports in *Bhagavad-gītā* and *Śrīmad-Bhāgavatam*, Śrīla Prabhupāda emphasizes that enviousness is the greatest problem facing the living entity. Śrīla Prabhupāda persistently states that the cause of our material bondage is our desire to usurp the Lord's position. Our incarceration in the material energy, which continues lifetime after lifetime as the process of *saṁsāra*, or repeated birth and death, is a direct result of coveting what belongs to Kṛṣṇa. Envy accompanies us as long as we carry material consciousness. The stronger the material consciousness, the stronger the envy we experience.

In his purport to *Śrīmad-Bhāgavatam* 3.15.19, Śrīla Prabhupāda writes that the most significant aspect of the spiritual world is its lack of envy. He explains that even the flowers and trees are not envious there. In other words, personalities in a seemingly lower *rasa*, or transcendental relationship with the Lord, neither resent those in different *rasas* nor others within the same *rasa*. From a materialistic point of view, we might think that those in *santa-rasa*, who are connected with the Lord in the mood of neutrality, or those in *dāsya-rasa*, whose eternal relationship with the Lord is one of servitorship, would feel jealous of those in *vātsalya-*, *sakhya-*, or *mādhurya-rasa*, who maintain parental, friendly, or conjugal relationships with the Lord, but actually such a mentality never arises. We want to free ourselves from that initial disease of enviousness towards Kṛṣṇa, which inevitably manifests in our daily relationships.

In the spiritual world, enviousness is conspicuous by its absence. Conversely, the most significant aspect of the material world is pervasive jealousy and discontent. Super-rich materialists may seem fortunate from the outside, but often internally they are miserable. Constantly, they find themselves confronted with people who are envious of what they possess. Wherever they go and whatever they do, both the rich and the famous are forced to move through environments in which people project their own negativity onto them. Those who are the most impious are the most envious. The demons want all of the opulences of the Lord without recognition of His supremacy. Just the mere idea of a Supreme is a botheration. Demons will aim to destroy anyone who seems to have a competitive edge.

Śrīla Prabhupāda Encounters Envy

During his travels, Śrīla Prabhupāda himself encountered enviousness in others. Occasionally, he suggested to his disciples that perhaps he should not sit on the *vyāsāsana*, or an elevated seat reserved for the spiritual master, because people would sometimes heckle him from the audience. Those genuinely looking for spiritual knowledge were not disturbed, sensing that Śrīla Prabhupāda was a superior person. They wanted to hear from him, but those who were envious could not appreciate the position of such a *sādhu*.

They merely became enraged when they encountered his superiority and wanted to know why he was sitting on such a large seat. While those not captured by envy could understand from his message the potency of his person, the minds of others could not accept that someone of a superior nature was speaking. As a result, they could not hear.

When we become willing to appreciate the achievement, excellence, or endowment of another person, then we will want to hear from them because we want to advance. But if we are envious, our growth will be blocked. Although we may find ourselves in the presence of a transcendental transmission, we will not hear the message if we are filled with resentment. We will merely allow ourselves to be distracted by the presentation, thinking of the speaker, "Who is he and why is he sitting there? I am not going to accept his position or what he is saying. Rather, I will challenge him." Envious people inevitably commit offenses, hurting themselves by missing the chance to hear.

When Śrīla Prabhupāda was manifest on this planet, he would sometimes ride in a Mercedes or a Rolls Royce in order to accept the service of those who wanted to serve him opulently. Noticing these luxury vehicles, ordinary people would sometimes become incensed. Having previously viewed the Hare Kṛṣṇas as hippies who dance in the streets, people in general immediately assumed that the opulence surrounding Śrīla Prabhupāda signified a sinister undertone to our movement. Due to enviousness, they were not ready to accept that someone who is close to God exists. Śrīla Prabhupāda is superior by his *adhikāra*, or level of spiritual advancement, and thus he is naturally someone whom others love and want to honor. In Philadelphia, a reporter challenged Śrīla Prabhupāda about the lavish transportation his disciples had arranged for him from the airport. Śrīla Prabhupāda explained that Kṛṣṇa's representative should be treated as good as God, teasing her gently by saying that "the car used at the airport was not sufficient; it should have been a gold car."*

Śrīla Prabhupāda dealt with people expertly, in many different ways, often charming them while delivering his transcendental message. Seeing the envy of his guests and wanting to transform it during a Vyāsa-pūjā discussion at New Vrindaban on September 2, 1972, Śrīla Prabhupāda humbly declared, "I am not perfect." Śrīla Prabhupāda emphasized that only because he was a carrier of perfect knowledge within a bona fide disciplic succession could he qualify to accept homage on behalf of the Lord.

Envy Prevents Us from Following Scripture

In *Bhagavad-gītā* 3.32, Kṛṣṇa says that those who do not regularly follow His teachings out of envy are to be considered bereft of all knowledge, befooled, and ruined in their endeavors for perfection. In his purport to *Bhagavad-gītā* 2.12, Śrīla Prabhupāda writes, "Those who are envious of Kṛṣṇa as the Supreme Personality of Godhead have no bona fide access to the great literature." A heart full of envy prevents us from being able to follow the scriptures. Those who harbor envy will not understand the scriptures; even if they understand to a degree, they will be unable to abide by them consistently. If we work at diminishing our envy, however, we stand a greater chance of being able to follow the process steadily.

Enviousness is the root cause of a consciousness of bondage. In his purport to *Śrīmad-Bhāgavatam* 4.19.2, which describes Lord Indra's envy of the sacrificial activities of Mahārāja Pṛthu, Śrīla Prabhupāda writes:

* Satsvarūpa dāsa Goswāmī, *Śrīla Prabhupāda Nectar*, Chapter Four

> *Since no one in this material world can tolerate another's advancement, everyone in the material world is called* matsara, *envious... [O]ne who is not free from the contamination of envy cannot advance in Kṛṣṇa consciousness. In Kṛṣṇa consciousness, however, if someone excels another person, the devotee who is excelled thinks how fortunate the other person is to be advancing in devotional service. Such nonenvy is typical of Vaikuṇṭha. However, when one is envious of his competitor, that is material.*

One can be engaged in the nine-fold process of devotional service, but it is all useless if one is contaminated by envy. Advancement means becoming free of envy, being unwilling to remain a slave of lust, greed, avariciousness, and egocentricity. It means developing Vaikuṇṭha consciousness—the mindset of the place where envy does not exist.

The *Śrīmad-Bhāgavatam* emphasizes that real nonviolence means freedom from envy. People normally equate violence with physical assault, but actually real violence constitutes any thought, word, or action that impedes the well-being of another. Envy means assault. It implies a violent attack. When we observe enviousness in ourselves or in another, we should immediately realize that this is a symptom of a very serious disease. Indra's biggest shortcoming is his envy. He is envious to such an extent that he tries to disrupt anyone engaged in austerity. He fears anyone who may become powerful enough to take away his own position. Even though he is an influential demigod, endowed with many potencies, Indra creates huge problems both for himself and for those he perceives as threats to his position.

Hiraṇyakaśipu, too, possessed tremendous power on a material level, but his most serious fault was envy of his five-year-old son, Prahlāda Mahārāja. Hiraṇyakaśipu envied Prahlāda because he was a pure devotee of the Lord. Demons like Hiraṇyakaśipu are very eager to annihilate God consciousness. They neither want to hear nor think about any aspects of Kṛṣṇa's glories. Merely glorifying Kṛṣṇa is an insult to the demons, what to speak of actually having a son who is fully engaged in transcendence. Extremely envious of both Kṛṣṇa and Prahlāda, who emanated Kṛṣṇa's potency, Hiraṇyakaśipu personifies everything that repels *bhakti.*

Similarly, Dakṣa was an expert Prajāpati, or one of the progenitors of mankind, but due to his envy of Lord Śiva, he had to suffer disastrous results. In his purport to *Śrīmad-Bhāgavatam* 4.4.23, in which Lord Śiva's wife Satī describes her disillusionment with her father Dakṣa, Śrīla Prabhupāda writes that "Dakṣa was the embodiment of envy, for he unnecessarily blasphemed a great personality, Lord Śiva." Although an elevated demigod, Dakṣa's snake-like behavior resulted in his daughter's decision to burn herself to ashes.

Envy Amongst Vaiṣṇavas

Being envious is one of the greatest *anarthas* because it sabotages the entire environment. Feeling envy communicates to others a subtle message of disempowerment. It implies that they should not do their service or, at best, that they should do it poorly so as to avoid becoming the target of negativity. If we allow ourselves to act on these negative messages, then the result is less service to Kṛṣṇa and *guru*, both in terms of quality and quantity. As Vaiṣṇavas, we should keep in mind that envy is comparable to telling another devotee, "Don't excel spiritually!" To a devotee who is singing nice *bhajanas,* or spiritual songs, in the temple, an envious person is actually saying, "Don't sing so beautifully for Kṛṣṇa!" When a *pūjārī* dresses the deities gorgeously, an envious person sends him the message, "Don't dress Kṛṣṇa so sweetly!" If we become envious of someone because they cook expertly for the deities, we basically communicate, "Don't offer Kṛṣṇa such nice preparations! Offer Him tasteless food." How can a devotee think in that way? "Offer *guru* poor quality, offer *sādhu* poor quality, offer Kṛṣṇa poor quality!" When we carry an envious mentality into the environment, we support mediocrity. The envious wish upon others: "Be whimsical and frivolous in your service."

The mentality of a real Vaiṣṇava is the opposite, of course. True devotees always want to see better service being done for Kṛṣṇa. They constantly examine their own lives to see how they can do more wonderful service for Kṛṣṇa and then meditate on how others can also do the same or better. We want to honor *bhakti* wherever we see it. Let us become exhilarated and enthused to see others with *bhakti*. We want to become motivated to excel personally, to supercede our own achievements. We could even aspire to go beyond the accomplishments of others, but in a non-envious way.

Recalling a conversation between King Nimi and the nine Yogendras in *Śrīmad-Bhāgavatam*, Canto 11, Chapter 2, Nārada Muni explains to Vasudeva that Vaiṣṇavas relate differently to those in superior, inferior, or equal positions to themselves. When someone is in a superior position, Śrī Nārada explains, we should open ourselves to receiving instructions from him or her. Of course, an envious person will never see anyone as superior; therefore, it is very difficult for such a person to accept instructions on how to improve. However, those who have an intense hunger to grow in Kṛṣṇa consciousness will treat other Vaiṣṇavas with proper respect and will be eager to hear from them. Wherever glorification of Kṛṣṇa occurs, a devotee wants to grab the opportunity to participate.

Relating to Juniors

At least three possible scenarios could take place when we interact with those who are so-called junior to us. In the first scenario, we reveal our envy of them by refusing to assume our responsibility to assist them. We may feel self-satisfied in the knowledge that they are in a lower position. In fact, we may desire to keep them in that position, realizing that if we give our help, they might come up to or even exceed our own so-called superior position. If we refuse to assist because we do not feel any inclination or any compassion, then we should be aware that we are in the mode of ignorance. We may feel enthused to know that those in a lesser position to us are not a part of the competition, and may even seek to see them fall even lower. In the second scenario, we are aware of our own advantageous position and are desirous of helping others by pulling them up. Just as a teacher feels fulfilled when a child is able to understand the lesson and apply it, so too a devotee becomes content when those junior to them make advancement. Any good teacher is eager to pull a student up and even happier when that student becomes a high achiever, perhaps even surpassing them. There is little or no envy in such a situation.

In the third scenario, the Vaiṣṇava is the servant of the servant. Instead of just pulling another up, the Vaiṣṇava goes underneath to push someone else up, even at the risk of jeopardizing his own position. This Vaiṣṇava's position far surpasses the first scenario in which someone in a higher position ignores someone in a lower position. For a genuine devotee, there is no question of ignoring others because he or she feels their miseries. This rare Vaiṣṇava also goes beyond the second scenario of merely pulling another up. The humanitarian or religionist will pull someone up because they are aware of their own superiority and want to help another based on that feeling. For instance, in India, where the vestiges of Vedic culture still exist, most people will give something to a traveling mendicant. However, generally they are motivated to assist him because doing so reinforces their own position of economic superiority. But genuine Vaiṣṇavas care so much that they are prepared to sacrifice their own greater position and stability. They will risk everything to help another.

Normally, people are not ready to help another. If they do help, they will only make the effort if it does not inconvenience them. They will assist only if it will not disturb their own egocentricity and individuality. Then they can tolerate the idea of extending themselves and giving their mercy, as and when they desire. Or they can tolerate the idea of giving to their subordinates because it reinforces their own position of superiority. Enviousness means focusing on what is constantly happening to me, for me, by me, and about me. Within this paradigm, "you" has very little significance to "me". Only if "you" are bothering "me" in some way does the "I" pay attention.

Generally, we do not mind extending ourselves if doing so reminds us of our pre-eminence. Our help is still somewhat condescending and void of the deep compassion which inspires one to make sacrifices. Kṛṣṇa is pleased when a person makes conscientious sacrifices without being foolish as she glorifies Him and shares what she has received. He explains that one who preaches to His devotees is most dear to Him. As we study this amazing position of selflessness, we see that the deeper the devotion and compassion, the less envy a person has in the heart. If we consistently endeavor with sacrifice, envy will diminish to a point at which we are able to be fully attentive to the needs and well-being of another.

Relating to Equals

A Vaiṣṇava never thinks that he is equal to another Vaiṣṇava, even when he has a relationship on the level of friendship. What normally happens in a material or a pseudo-spiritual situation is that friends simply come together to brag and focus the attention on themselves. When the friendship is not deep, envy will surface within both parties. As both come together in so-called friendship, boasting about all their achievements in the past and the present, they merely become more and more envious of each other.

When we examine various occupations, we discover that people in similar fields envy one another more than those in other careers. For instance, a painter will not be as envious of an excellent carpenter as he would be of another painter who excels. Someone who is a great architect will not necessarily be as envious of a doctor as she would of another architect because the doctor's achievements do not enter into her life space. The doctor's success is not as relevant to her existence. Unfortunately, instead of mutual appreciation of excellence arising in a particular field, or profound bonding based on certain achievements, usually the opposite happens. When we hear of the success of another person in our line of work, do we become distressed, even morbid? Some people become depressed when they see others excel. And sadly, people will engage in all kinds of negative activities to try to keep others down.

When people visit their friends or relatives, it is natural for them to inquire about one another's well-being. If a friend replies by telling us how wonderful his life has been lately, the other person might smile, but think privately, "Why is life so good for you? I thought I would have been far ahead of you by now." Or she may think, "I have always been more successful than you, but now you're catching up with me!" These perverse thoughts develop due to enviousness.

Instead of relishing the achievements of another, the opposite occurs. When friends in the same class see one of their group attain a score higher than everybody else, they frequently become disturbed. Each thinks to himself or herself, "This person is detracting from my position as the most wonderful, intelligent, attractive, or strong." Again, this mentality is part of the demonic consciousness of wanting to hijack the opulences of Kṛṣṇa, to usurp the position of the Supreme.

As opposed to superficial relationships, a deep, genuine friendship will not be affected by unhealthy competitiveness; rather, each friend feels a real sense of concern for the other's well-being, an authentic sense of happiness seeing the other fulfilling his or her potential.

Envy Means Violence

One of the biggest problems in the workplace and in politics is that people feel they should be careful of what they say and do. They anticipate trouble, sensing they must watch their backs. Someone else is always envious of them. Afraid that a coworker might outshine them, they defensively guard their position. How many of us have lost jobs because a coworker sabotaged us? Real nonviolence means freedom from envy. Being envious means violence to the highest degree. It means desiring the demise of another. Not only do his achievements become a botheration to us, but we want his very existence to come to an end. No sane person envies a failure or a low achiever. We are envious of those who excel in some way. We view others' accomplishments as ones which should belong to us.

In your own life, you may notice that if you are very envious of certain people, you do not want to see them, to hear about them, or to be around those who talk about them. The stronger the envy, the more we desire their annihilation.

Similarly, demons want to destroy anything theistic. Most of us are aware that certain situations elicit enviousness more than others. Therefore, as devotees, we should be mindful to act in such a way as to minimize agitating the minds of the demons, the atheists, and the pseudo-spiritualists. At the same time, we must communicate the message as Kṛṣṇa desires despite the fact that people may become envious and disturbed. Māyāvādīs, or those who believe they can become God, exhibit so much envy because they do not want to accept the personal expression of God. It is our duty to preach that Kṛṣṇa is the ultimate controller. Each individual soul, captured by the unfolding of his or her *karma*, is guaranteed a predetermined amount of happiness and distress. Many people find it difficult to accept that they are not quite as wonderful as they think. Therefore, we must be tactful while communicating the truth. If we tell a member of the public, "Sir, judging by the way you're living, you may not even come back to the human platform," he will simply become agitated as most people think that their wealth, opulence, or assets guarantee them security.

Occasionally, dangerous people join a spiritual society in order to discover the secrets of obtaining power and becoming worshipable. In a similar but less extreme way, devotees with varying degrees of sincerity sometimes take to the renounced order of life because they observe the external benefits that accompany such a position. And of course, such a mentality is accompanied by inherent dynamite which is going to explode at some point. If we are motivated more by the desire to enjoy or control than to serve when we accept a position in a spiritual hierarchy, then we demonstrate very clearly that we still want to usurp the position of Kṛṣṇa. In this case, power becomes a source of entanglement rather than liberation: instead of increasing our spiritual acceleration, our position becomes more and more the cause of our incarceration in the material world.

Introspection Is Vital

Let us constantly introspect. Search inwardly to see how Kṛṣṇa gives us so many chances to advance, to perceive more clearly exactly what kinds of diseases infect us. If we observe recurring expressions of enviousness in the devotee community, then we know we have a problem of epidemic proportions. When devotees attack one another, they are really suggesting that Kṛṣṇa, *guru*, and *sādhus* should not be served. Impersonalists also do not want to serve Kṛṣṇa. Demons not only resist serving, but hate Kṛṣṇa. Neither impersonalists nor demons want to have anything to do with Kṛṣṇa, nor do they want to be in the proximity of anyone who is connected with Him. As we discover some level of enviousness arising in whatever situation we find ourselves, whether it is with a superior, a peer, or a so-called junior, we should realize, "Oh, these are some of the reasons why I am a conditioned soul. This explains why I'm not advancing and feeling more enthusiastic and having more realizations, why I'm not becoming free from sense gratification. This disease is eating away at my consciousness." We want to go beyond just acknowledging the problem, to exceed even the pious gesture of reaching down to pull someone up. Ultimately, we want to be so concerned that others get help that we go behind them and push, even though it may put a little more pressure on us. Our actions may even put us in a position of being their inferior, but such is our concern for others that we are joyful to see them excelling as we push them forward. Then we notice we are moving with them as we take care to place them in the topmost position.

Question: I have heard that one of the best ways of dealing with envy, especially amongst the Vaiṣṇavas, is to serve those of whom we are envious. But sometimes it is not possible to serve them directly because, for instance, they might live far away. Is there an alternative way to rid ourselves of envy?

Answer: You can always serve. Even if you cannot serve others in person, you can send a letter, a card, or a gift, or arrange in some way to do something as an expression of honoring that person's existence. Be creative. Enviousness means attacking another's existence. Therefore, freedom from envy means doing the opposite. Find ways to appreciate the presence of those around you, to serve them and to honor them. Celebrating another's existence has nothing to do with geography or circumstance. It is not necessary to be physically near another in order to celebrate them. In fact, sometimes we may discover our enviousness is so strong that it's unhealthy to have much direct association with the person we envy, because we may not be able to control ourselves. But as we work on those feelings at a distance, serving humbly, we will find alleviation.

At times, when people have been combative over protracted issues, the energy between them may be too intense to allow immediate resolution to take place. Even when one or both parties want to resolve the situation, meeting incites too many bad reflections and the enmity between them just cannot be put to rest. Therefore, sometimes the combatants have to work at solving their problems at a distance, perhaps working through an arbitrator or another conducive medium which facilitates healing. Similarly, if you find you cannot serve directly for whatever reason, then find some way to enhance the well-being of the one whom you envy, because without a doubt, your envy means an attack on his or her well-being.

Question: Devotees are generally kind-hearted because of their desire to know and serve Kṛṣṇa, but sometimes we find that we're hurt by what another devotee may say or do to us. How should we deal with those feelings?

Answer: We're not voidists or impersonalists. Therefore, naturally we have personality and feelings. Generally in Vaiṣṇava culture, however, feelings of hurt and outrage are usually triggered due to an offense towards another Vaiṣṇava rather than to ourselves. A high-level devotee becomes very disturbed when they hear someone belittling a great saint, the *guru*, or the deities, but when they hear the same blasphemy about themselves, they remain unruffled. When someone insults us, we should be ready to accept the situation as an opportunity for growth. If someone tells us, "*Prabhu*, your chanting is horrible," we should thank them and see how to improve, even though we may be chanting the clearest, most focused rounds in the temple. If someone else tells us that we fold our sari so poorly, we can thank them and ask, "Can you show me how I can do better?" If someone criticizes our *sādhana* or service, we do not have to become disturbed, but rather we should see how to improve.

If someone attacks our personality, we should take the opportunity to look a little closer at why we are getting so upset. Is there perhaps some truth in what they have said? Even if someone attacks our personality unjustifiably, we should feel sorry for them, because they are not only hurting their own devotional life but degrading the atmosphere. If we do not care about them sufficiently, we will think, "Why did they say that to me?" We should feel hurt that another Vaiṣṇava is not sufficiently using the process, thus cheating him or herself out of a superior situation. Real Vaiṣṇavas are happy when others are accelerating in devotional life.

If others are sabotaging themselves, we should feel sad for them and not for ourselves.

Why does Śrīla Haridāsa Ṭhākura plead with the Lord for those who beat him in twenty-two market places to be exonerated? He felt no anger, only compassion. Why did Śrī Kūreśa beg his deity of Śrī Varadarāja not only for the forgiveness but for the liberation of those who blinded him? It's counterproductive to allow ourselves to be captured by the comments people may make about our bodies and our personalities. Someone playing the "body game" or the "personality game" reveals a consciousness which is entangled in the material energy. Why should we allow ourselves to be disturbed when someone else lowers their own consciousness by playing material games? If we do not access sufficient devotion or strength, or are captured by enviousness ourselves, then we will be caught by the lower modes and we will be dragged down too. If someone insults a billionaire, saying, "You are a pauper! You have nothing," do you think she will lose any sleep over those remarks? But if in fact she has borrowed someone else's fancy car and someone says, "I know that is not yours," then she will grow angry. A pretentious person will feel disturbed when he is insulted, because he wants everyone to think that he is wonderful. But if we are actually devotees, then we just feel sad because someone else is trying to destroy us instead of focusing on improving the quality of their own devotion.

Question: Mahārāja, in your talk you equated enviousness with the feeling that we deserve the opulences someone else exhibits, opulences which ultimately belong to Kṛṣṇa. But is it not good to be desirous of acquiring the positive qualities we see in other devotees, even if we may be a little envious?

Answer: What you have pointed out is the disparity between genuinely appreciating the wonderful abilities and attributes we notice in another devotee, and wanting to steal them from him because we think ourselves more deserving. That is the difference. In the first case, we honor someone else's existence to the point that we would like to emulate their behavior and achievements, while in the second case, we are antagonistic towards them and desire to eradicate not only their achievements but their very presence. We are always to seek out higher association, to find those who inspire us to greater depths of *bhakti*, but when we encounter them, we are to support them in a humble mood instead of desiring their demise.

Question: Although I have so many *anarthas* and I feel so inferior in comparison with other devotees, sometimes they come and ask me for assistance. But I feel that I have nothing to offer due to my position. How is it possible for me to serve the devotees?

Answer: We do not have to refrain from service because we feel inferior. As a matter of fact, a menial consciousness of being the servant makes us even more eager to assist, even though we may be so unqualified. When we say "*prabhu*," we are really conveying the understanding that "you're my master and I am here to serve you." You cannot look upon another devotee as your master and still feel superior. We are supposed to think that others have a greater claim on Kṛṣṇa's mercy than we do, that they are greater recipients than ourselves. Therefore, we look upon service to them as a chance to gain more of Kṛṣṇa's mercy. To our detriment, we fail to recognize the potency of unmotivated, uninterrupted service to the Supreme.

Usually, we serve because someone likes us and we like them and therefore we want to assist them. If someone does not like us very much, we are not really inspired to serve them. If someone listens to us, then we like that person, but if someone else does not, then we have no time for that individual. This is all material consciousness. You can learn sometimes more from those whom you dislike or with whom you disagree than from those with whom you do get along or who agree with you. Frequently, a person who likes you will be reluctant to point out difficult issues, because in most cases the relationship is superficial, and they want to hold on to your superficial friendship. Someone who is not your so-called friend may reveal information that can be most helpful. An actual Vaiṣṇava does not categorize friends separately from enemies.

Chapter 3

Loving Our Neighbors More Than Ourselves

The Necessary Preparation

Whenever we plan to change locations, even for a few hours, we generally need to make preparations according to the exact nature of the new environment. If we are going to a formal event, then we make sure we are dressed in suitable attire. Similarly, when artists intend to perform for an audience, they usually practice rigorously beforehand. Concerned about the quality of their rendition, artists understand that if they are not properly prepared, they will simply be embarrassed by an incoherent performance when it is time to mount the stage.

We, too, all have some place to go. All the major scriptures emphasize that we have a home situated far beyond the mundane reality in which we find ourselves temporarily. All the major scriptures underline the fact that we are eternal, but as we look at our lives, we cannot help but realize that everything is relative. This impermanence indicates that we are out of place. Therefore, we want to prepare ourselves to regain what we have lost, to receive the marvelous treasures that await us. Moving expediently towards that goal entails an adjustment in mental orientation which aligns the physical with a Higher Power.

Breaking Free of Materialism

Such a shift in consciousness is particularly significant in an environment of gross materialism, in which the basic mindset is one of simply conquering over nature, rather than harmoniously co-existing. The basic cultural rule today is: "Every man and every woman for themselves. Do whatever you think is best for you. Don't worry about the consequences; just become expert at getting away with whatever pleases you." When the general consciousness of everyone is "each for themselves," then even the concept of God becomes less and less of a consideration.

Since we are constantly trying to manipulate and dominate, we keep putting ourselves in all kinds of misery. Spiritual realization is not something that is imposed from without, but rather lies dormant within each one of us. Outside involvements are to help us access greater faith and clarity about how to more fully experience what we already have. Somehow or other, we have covered over our true nature by superfluous things.

Frequently running away from those people and circumstances that are most beneficial to us, we experience a form of insanity called materialism. Constantly capturing the senses, materialism force-feeds one constantly with irrelevant situations. Masquerading as physical or emotional nourishment, these situations are generally detrimental, lulling us into the illusion that everything is okay, while in fact we are being poisoned. Arranged by advertising agencies and sponsors, most fads are extremely destructive to our well-being, but because so many people participate in them, we also may absorb ourselves in current trends.

Peer pressure has a big effect on everyone. However, as we are less concerned with false ego, distinction, adoration, and temporary profits, we will not be as captivated by unhealthy patterns as we were previously.

Anyone who has ever made a serious contribution in this world was not afraid to be different. Most attained success by pursuing a particular idea they believed in, despite the awareness that they were flouting convention. If we are too cowardly to launch ahead with love and devotion, or if we are too afraid of being different, that is most unfortunate, as the norm of this world is one of insane patterns. The number one business in the western world is arguably the Pentagon, an organization literally designed to conduct accelerated attacks on other countries. How healthy is a culture which has produced enough chemical and nuclear weaponry to annihilate every man, woman, and child on the planet—many, many times? How well-meaning is a society which uses its greatest minds and financial resources to perfect the ability to kill others?

When the majority of the citizens of a particular sovereign power accept deviations from the natural flow of life as the normal culture, it signifies that the government is seriously defective. The government functions like a teacher. In a classroom situation, if many students are insubordinate, then we will naturally look to the teacher for clarification. We will question whether the teacher has implemented proper techniques of caring, of creating an exhilarating atmosphere of inquiry in the consciousness of her dependents. If she has implemented the appropriate teaching methods, and leads by example, then generally students will behave correctly. If, however, the teacher does not function as a proper role model and does not care about the students, then her actions will produce negative results.

Sadly, teenagers today commit more crimes than adults. As the youth are the future, our environment is increasingly filled with people who feel angry and frustrated, and therefore frequently lash out at others. Trying to be a normal part of an insane environment is the real insanity. Desiring to counter such insanity in a God-conscious way according to bona fide scripture, we assume a healthy, thoughtful position.

Compassion Is the Key

Excerpts from a meditation in my book, *The Beggar I* (entitled *Compassion Is the Key*), follow shortly. My intention when writing this meditation was to assist in triggering the shift in mental orientation required for entering into the selfless transcendental abode of the Supreme Lord. Certain orthodox scriptures such as the Bible, the Koran, and the Torah highlight the commandment that "We should love our neighbors as ourselves." While this is a wonderful aspiration, is it not even more powerful to love your neighbor over and beyond the value you place on your own mind and body? That is transcendental. In fact, to use ourselves as a referent for everything is a form of craziness.

As we are all products of heredity and environmental considerations to some extent, aspiring to love our neighbors as ourselves may result in a business-like mentality by which we may refuse to let our love flow if our neighbor does not reciprocate accordingly. But if we attempt to arrange as much or even more for others than we do for ourselves, then the universe will supply us with an incredible amount of support, much more than we ourselves would attract normally. Not only will we attract an abundance of everything we need, but the Lord and the Lord's agents cannot fail to come to our call due to our selfless alignment with a higher consciousness. In such a consciousness, we are no longer controlled by the normal stagnations of this particular realm. As we develop that higher perception and higher love, we find that we are no longer enlisted in the environment of imprisonment. We discover, with increasing surprise and joy, that we are already categorized as those who will receive spiritual boons, as those who will be paroled from this cold prison-like atmosphere of confusion and chastisement.

The theme for this meditation is straightforward: without the most profound compassion, no one can enter into the kingdom of God. I wrote in a personal way, addressing the Lord as He gives attention to the aspirant who humbly approaches Him through the agency of the spiritual master. Try to visualize the scheme of activities required to make a profound shift in consciousness. Firstly, understand the kind of consciousness and sacrifice required to go back to the kingdom of God. Secondly, literally make an appeal to the Lord to be uplifted, to be brought back. And thirdly, understand that the spiritual master is a mentor or prophet-like figure whom the Lord has summoned to assist us in connecting with His kingdom. The spiritual master helps the wandering soul know what is to be done and how it is to be done. He empowers us to be able to do the necessary—if we will only let him.

Yesterday, my dear Lord Syāma, I tried to make an appeal to You.

I inquired, "Dear Lord, since I have been away from You for so long, trying to do Your work in the material worlds, don't You think it is time for me to return home, back to Your divine abode?"

You glanced at me in a penetrating and loving way, and instead of being angry with me for my presumptuous and arrogant nature, You, out of great concern, asked my spiritual master to enlighten me.

Frequently, we demand from God so much more than what we are truly worthy of, begging for new situations in which we could not perform adequately anyway, even if they were to manifest. We demand the world but want to give almost nothing in return. Although we desire many blessings, we inconsistently execute those activities that will qualify us as candidates to receive an abundance of unconditional love.

My spiritual master said, "My dear son, please come with me. See that blind man stumbling around, trying to move about as people are bumping into him? When your compassion is so strong for this soul that you are ready to take his place, freeing him from his torment, then you will be a candidate for the kingdom of God."

As I studied the blind man's condition, I was overwhelmed with compassion.

Sometimes, we fail to realize how difficult life can be for the visually impaired. Our entire world is oriented for sighted people. Most of us categorize our world based on visual perceptions. Without sight, one is forced to depend heavily on the environment or on others for clarification and identification. In that desperate state of helplessness, others may ignore or even abuse us. Here the spiritual master challenges the candidate, "Oh, so you want to go back to God? You want to develop proper love? You want to become anti-material, to acquire the consciousness necessary to associate with residents who are pure beings of love?" He escorts the candidate around secular environments, showing him or her possibilities of transcending the aspiration of merely loving the neighbor as oneself.

Entering the Anti-Material Realm

When one is ready to make a sacrifice so that someone else can be relieved of their discomfort, even if it means jeopardizing one's own sense of security, then one enters the anti-material realm. A material mindset basically means a struggle for survival, resulting in victory for those who are experts in manipulating others. A spiritual mindset is the opposite of the material because it reflects a platform which is free of enviousness and proprietorship, based ultimately on unmotivated, unconditional love. Making sacrifices on behalf of one's beloved, or even on behalf of a stranger—not begrudgingly or out of guilt or fear, but out of compassion—reflects true love.

If we are honest with ourselves, we will acknowledge that often we serve others with great reluctance. In our hearts, we do not really want to assist them, but because we find ourselves in compelling circumstances, we do what others want only because we have not yet found a way to avoid helping them. But when one caters to others with an exhilarated consciousness, out of true compassion and concern, then one will experience great bliss.

> *The spiritual master said, "My dear son, please come with me. Observe this man who has impaired speech. There are so many things he would like to talk about and express to others, but since he cannot talk, he is usually disregarded, and this leaves the poor man in great frustration. When you are ready to take his place so he can be freed of his torment, then you will be a candidate for the kingdom of God."*

As I studied the man's condition, I was overwhelmed with compassion.

The spiritual master requested that I continue with him. He said, "Please observe the invalid confined to his bed. Notice how he is a burden to his so-called friends and family members. They will be so relieved when he finally dies."

Those who have been placed in situations in which they are confined and are forced to depend on others to feed them, to bathe them, and sometimes even to take them to the toilet will know how humbling this experience can be. The caregivers often see the lifestyle of the invalid as an imposition on themselves.

When your compassion is so strong for this soul that you are ready to take his place so he can be freed from his torment, then you will be a candidate for the kingdom of God."

As I studied the invalid's condition, I was overwhelmed with compassion.

The spiritual master motioned, "Come this way, my beloved son. Take notice of this homeless man. At the end of the day, he has no family or home to return to, and even when he tries to find a place to rest, sometimes the children harass him or the police arrest him. When your compassion is so strong for this soul that you are ready to take his place so he can be freed from his torment, then you will be a candidate for the kingdom of God."

As I studied the homeless man and his condition, I was overwhelmed with compassion.

Truly Feeling for Others

In Raghunātha dāsa Gosvāmī's *Vilāpa-kusumāñjali* (6), we hear, *kṛpāmbudhir yaḥ para-duḥkha-duḥkhī*, that the *sādhu* literally feels both the happiness and the misery of others. Therefore, he or she is very careful not to give anyone pain, and very enlivened when someone else experiences a joyful moment. Sometimes people secretly feel happy to see someone else in misery. They feel better about their own lives when they notice that another's condition is worse than their own. Let us look within and see how this paradigm manifests in our own lives. Occasionally, when something negative happens to a friend, although we may utter words of condolence, in our inner consciousness, we may actually be grateful that it happened to them and not us.

If we introspect, we will notice that at times we feel a sense of well-being knowing that our position is seemingly better than someone else's. Meditating thus, we immerse ourselves in the material paradigm. Being spiritual means that one genuinely feels the misery, the pain, the misfortune of another as one's own. Spiritual consciousness means becoming attentive to the inner reality of others. Not only do we try not to inflict pain upon another, but we become alert to his or her suffering, devising ways to relieve it.

Try to visualize the torment that others immersed in awful situations are forced to undergo. Meditate on the kind of love needed to willingly accept their particular lot. If we are cowards, we cannot think about assuming another's despair. To make such a compassionate action requires not mere religiosity, but a deep level of spirituality. Readiness to make any sacrifice in order to raise the level of consciousness on the planet requires immense spiritual maturity and a powerful sense of spiritual warriorship.

Gratitude Increases Compassion

Gratitude for what we have helps us to take less for granted. Occasionally, it is healthy for us to walk through environments of extreme despair. Although some of us feel much frustration and anxiety daily, we would complain less if we became aware of the millions of people whose conditions are far worse than ours have ever been in this lifetime. Yes, we gripe about discomforts and inconveniences, but at the end of the day we have food to eat and a roof over our heads. Some of us grumble that we cannot make our car payments, but at least we have cars to drive. Many of us moan that we struggle to pay our insurance, but we are insured. It is helpful to remind ourselves that the majority of people on this planet do not have access to such facilities. Many countries in the world do not have any welfare systems. If a person is handicapped or unemployed, he simply has to beg. If someone lacks a family to take care of them, they may starve. We moan about issues which interfere with our basic day-to-day pleasures, rather than matters which literally concern life or death.

Have you considered interrupting your normal schedule once in a while to visit a hospital? Walk the floors a couple of times. Notice that many people are bed-ridden and have tubes coming out of them. Visit a mental institution or a school for the visually-challenged or hearing-impaired. We gripe more than we thank the Lord for the abundance He has given us. Why do we not work harder at using what we have to make a difference for others instead? An attitude of sacrifice will empower us to uplift the atmosphere of stagnation prevalent on the planet.

The spiritual master asked me to take notice of a refugee family. They lived like wild animals roaming from one dangerous situation to another. Looking for food, shelter, and security, even though they were not behind bars, they were imprisoned by their desperate condition. In great fear they tried to shake off the past, moving from city to city and camp to camp. Their release would come only from death, which stalked their every step.

Most of us have never experienced a war situation in which people have to abandon everything that they have spent their entire lives acquiring. They may even have been forced to leave behind those who are most dear to them. Many refugees have seen their loved ones slaughtered right in front of them. Those of us who have lost a loved one will understand that sometimes we never fully recover from this experience. Forced to live with traumatic memories while they have nothing secure to depend upon, millions of survivors of ethnic clashes around the world naturally fear the future. Sometimes, survivors lose the desire to live. Children especially suffer in these kinds of conflicts. Imagine being in a situation in which the world, as you know it, is gone, and those whom you love the most are scattered, lost, or dead. The dire truth is that wars break out everywhere, not only on this planet, but throughout the entire universe.

My spiritual master repeated, "When your compassion, my dear son, is so strong for these souls that you are willing to take their place so they can be freed from their torment, then you will be a candidate for the kingdom of God"

As I studied their pitiful predicament, I was overwhelmed with compassion.

Depth of Compassion Indicates Advancement

Spiritual advancement is directly proportionate to the depth of our compassion and our ability to love. Highly empowered beings develop such an intense desire to make a dramatic change in people's lives that the Lord empowers them, enabling them to achieve results far beyond their own capacities. Great prophets in many traditions exemplify this phenomenon. Some have been sent as ambassadors from higher abodes. They send out signals that will attract those who are ready to respond to the call for freedom. Other prophets come directly from the communities of this world. Feeling the severe pain of the suffering multitudes, their depth of compassion inspires the Lord to empower them as His agencies. One of the greatest accomplishments for a person in this state of evolution is to make his consciousness and body available to the higher powers, despite the fact that he may still be conditioned. Surrendering one's free will to the Lord means the eradication of not just our own karmic patterns, but also those of others. Lord Jesus Christ was one such compassionate being who absorbed the collective *karma* of millions. By literally dying for the sins of humankind, Lord Jesus gave others the valuable opportunity to understand higher truths, to open up doors for various agents of the Lord to make contact.

This environment is so heavily constricted by the modes of material nature that it is as if we are bound by many ropes and chains. Great teachers come to sever some of these bonds so that people may have a chance to know the truth. Most of us are blissfully unaware of the many negative forces that bombard us every day. Some environments are so sinful that even if we desire a higher consciousness, it becomes incredibly difficult for us to think and act differently. Elevated beings play a major role in removing some of these thick coverings. In making sacrifices for humanity, they allow us to exercise our free will fully. While it is still up to us how we use our free will, these exalted souls create an atmosphere which facilitates a superior freedom of choice. These meditations are designed to help us cultivate a mindset which can allow God to empower us. This empowerment will sustain us as we prepare to engage in spiritual warfare. A soldier who goes out today to do combat without proper weaponry will merely become a casualty. Forces of oppression can quickly bring one to a state of devastation if one is not properly equipped, especially if one cannot draw on adequate reinforcements.

The spiritual master encouraged me to observe the situation of a helpless child who was being repeatedly abused by those who were supposed to be her protectors. This innocent child kept turning to her parents and others for love and protection, but all they gave her was more abuse. The little child, unfortunately, perceived the entire world as a hostile place where adults existed just to inflict pain upon her.

"Here again, my son, I must stress to you that when your compassion is so strong for this soul that you are willing to take her place so she can be freed from this torment, then you will be a candidate for the kingdom of God."

Selfishness Keeps Us Imprisoned

True spirituality has nothing to do with salvation. Studying *yoga* techniques, going to church or temple once a week, or gaining psychic powers are simply elementary means to cope with this environment of imprisonment. Attempts to find relief from the anxiety of life have very little to do with actual liberation, with what awaits us beyond this world of selfishness. With so much self-centeredness, we cannot develop a highly spiritual consciousness, nor can we go back to the kingdom of God. If we are serious about returning home, we must constantly take inventory of ourselves. What is the focus of our days? Most of the time, we concentrate our energies on satisfying our wants and desires. We allow ourselves to be captured by the many objects which are constantly put before us, objects which, in most cases, we do not even need. Programmed to pursue external objects, we have allowed ourselves to become distracted from experiencing deep love and true happiness, from feeling a sense of constant well-being. Usually, we are so connected to the paradigm of duality that although we strive to access a higher reality, after a short while we fall back into constantly feeding the senses. Imbalanced easily, we return to our comfortable consciousness of "I" and "mine."

I did not have time to compose myself, when my spiritual master said, "Once more, please come with me. Regard this elderly lady. She has given her life to her friends and family, but now that she has grown old and wrinkled, no one wants to even look at her withered face. Even the smallest request from her causes such resentment that they frequently beat her. Her family members are worse than vultures. They take her money and other assets, hoping all the while that she will soon die so that they can be through with her once and for all."

The spiritual master turned to look at me with tear-filled eyes. I had not realized how much he too had been moved by the sufferings of all these souls. The tears ran more profusely down his face as he said with a choked-up voice, "When you have such compassion for these tormented souls that you not only are willing to change places with them, but are eagerly willing to remain in this hellish planet eternally, giving up all the credits you have earned to be used by others; when you are willing to give up all considerations for your own liberation so that these souls can be liberated—only then can you be considered a serious candidate to return home back to the kingdom of God."

One who is actually a high-level servant of God surrenders to Him with intense selflessness in order to attract His help in uplifting the planet. Such deep commitment and compassion purchase the Lord, summoning His loving assistance in activating a serious change. Of course, the Lord will not allow one of His dear servants to suffer eternally for others. But a real willingness to absorb another's pain is an impetus for ultimate absorption into the environment of ever-increasing love.

Willingness to compassionately accept the pain of another is not reflected in the conception of God as an order supplier to whom we go just for our daily bread. Neither is it found amongst those who conceive of spiritual life as an extracurricular affair, who attempt to be religious because they are afraid that if they are not religious, they may be chastised. High-level spirituality is not about what God can do for you. Rather, it is about you trying to make a change in your own consciousness so that you can do something significant for the Lord and for the world.

Selflessness Empowers Us Unlimitedly

The enormous problems and sufferings of these people were overwhelming to me. I thought: Is it possible for any person to have such profound, selfless compassion? But, before I could express this in words, I looked again at my guru's *face and I realized how fortunate I was, for standing before me, guiding me, was such a selfless glorious soul. I knew he would gladly forego all personal concerns to guarantee the return of other souls to the kingdom of God.*

There was nothing left for me to say or do other than to promise the spiritual master that I would not rest until I had developed such profound compassion. Such compassion is not possible without serious blessings from the guru *and other souls, so I beg for their blessings. Other than that I will be forced to remain a pseudo-devotee. I beg that you make me such a pure devotee, although I am most unworthy.*

Overall, this reflection addresses the anti-material consideration of going beyond the conception of "I" and "mine," which surpasses notions of salvation, and especially notions of material comfort and security. One also rejects the pursuit of mystic powers, abandoning thinking of one's own well-being in every situation. At the same time, one is extremely sensitive to the misfortune of others, literally feeling their suffering as one's own. As we genuinely feel others' pain, we become dedicated to actively relieving it. Such souls who genuinely desire to alleviate others' suffering will become highly empowered. Considering the massive problems facing the world, very powerful generals and spiritual soldiers are needed to move through the normal levels of contamination and to assist the suffering masses genuinely. These empowered devotees of the Lord can uplift many people who go to bed in misery and wake up in misery. These devotees can enable anyone to become hopeful by conveying God's love to them.

Question: What if others do not have a desire to receive what we have to give?

Answer: High spiritual technology allows one to help those who consciously make themselves available, as well as those who do not. Purity of purpose affects people subconsciously. Of course, the element of free will is always present. One respects it and does not force oneself on another, but nevertheless endeavors humbly to assist. Sometimes people are so confused and demoralized that they cannot see help when it is put in front of them. Either they have lost faith in everything, or they have become so distracted by negativity that even when they are given a chance to make a change for the better, they do not take advantage of it.

One of the biggest problems in the world today, more severe than the calamities with which we are constantly confronted, is the impotency of spiritual leaders. Both Western and Eastern philosophies acknowledge that people in general are mostly docile followers. They will adhere to fads and trends, imitating what their leaders and peers do. Therefore, the inability of spiritualists to hold back negative currents is a tremendous source of concern. Most spiritual leaders are devoid of the ability to arrange a higher intervention, a lacking which leaves people at the mercy of demonic arrangements.

In this type of environment, it is to be expected that people will not respond immediately when we try to assist. We should try to develop a love that is potent enough to engulf others, to carry them to a point at which they can perceive that we are their well-wishers. Most of us have been so disappointed in the past that we hold back, afraid of being cheated again. As we ourselves become consistently loving in such situations, then others cannot fail to respond as they see that our love is not based on exterior motivation. Everyone really wants the best for themselves. If we are truly convinced that someone is acting in our best interests, we will naturally open ourselves to that person, and try to act upon his or her guidance.

Question: I appreciate your analogy of a war to describe the challenges which will confront us as we endeavor to change our consciousness. How do we perform our duty as liberators when, at the same time, we are also prisoners of war?

Answer: First of all, realize that no one can give what they themselves do not have. Therefore, if we want to make a difference in the problems of society, we must start transforming ourselves first. The more we allow ourselves to be love in action and become fortified in transcendental understanding, the more we can share with others. As we connect with spiritual techniques, as we read, and as we chant, our meditation should be one of preparation for greater service to humanity. Instead of thinking about how we can enhance our own material situations or gain psychic leverage over others, we should try to grow so that we can uplift others. Compassion cannot exist without humility.

Humility does not mean that we are cowards and neglect our responsibilities. Rather, it means that we are so concerned about others that we are ready to become agents of change. And not only do we not expect any rewards for our actions, we realize that we may even be denigrated for extending ourselves to assist others. Nevertheless, we are ready to make that sacrifice because we are humbly fixed on making a positive difference in our environment. Yes, your own love and devotion can make a powerful difference. Uplifting the environment begins with ourselves. Let us work on raising our own consciousness, but not in an egocentric manner. Working on the self is similar to the preparations a soldier makes before he or she enters the battlefield. A selfless mindset allows one access to higher realms.

Bear in mind that subtle influences are always more penetrating than external ones. As we interact with one another, we share not only hereditary and environmental factors from this lifetime, but karmic patterns from previous lifetimes embedded within our subtle bodies. However, patterns from this lifetime are generally more dominant in our consciousness. Since we interact on subtle levels, we sometimes do not have to do much on the physical plane. We can create an impact on the environment simply through our own higher awareness. Frequently, a little expression of genuine concern is as beneficial to those in need as the practical help which may accompany it. Notice how sometimes wealthy people will put a dollar into a homeless person's hand merely because they want to be rid of them, but many times the greatest gift is not even a physical gift, but the transfer of consciousness.

Very often, people accept degraded conditions because they have not experienced love. A large number of children today are hostile and violent due to the types of environments in which they are raised. It is almost impossible for them to act differently as they have been produced out of violence, not real love. The union that brought them into the world was usually self-centered and exploitive. While in the womb, they were subject to outbursts of aggression, anxiety, and despair and, after birth, they underwent similar negative experiences at critical ages. Such souls may never have been in contact with anyone who really cares, at least in this lifetime.

We sometimes hear stories of people who have overcome drug addictions or repeated criminal convictions to become productive members of society, often due to the influence of one person who made a difference in their lives. Previously bent on destroying themselves and others, these reformed criminals subsequently became effective politicians, teachers, and educators despite their background of violence. Remember that we all affect one another in different ways although we are often unaware of the degree to which we influence the environment. Especially today, when the normative patterns of life suffocate the citizens of the world, a little breath of fresh air can make a huge change, especially if it is potent. As we carry a greater sense of divinity within us, so are the contacts we make with others automatically of a higher quality.

The culture of imprisonment on the planet is increasing daily despite the fact that in many cities there are mosques, churches, synagogues, or temples on every other corner. There are many so-called religious people in the United States: in the Pledge of Allegiance we say "one nation under God"; on the dollar bill it is written "In God We Trust"; and even the President takes his oath on a Bible. Unfortunately, religion has become so mechanical that the real spiritual rule of law means very little. During a crisis, politicians will frequently appear on our television screens, exhorting somberly, "Let us pray to God." Usually, they have almost no faith in God, but they understand that this particular utterance captures the attention of the people and makes them feel a sense of security.

It is time for people to stop prostituting religion and to become truly spiritual. Furthermore, it is time for people to stop hiding behind institutions, which is just another form of sectarianism. It is time for people to stop doubting their own prophets and to stop interpreting what their prophets said and did. It is time to take the words of the prophets as a genuine spiritual connection and to live according to those great orthodox traditions, which have been given by divine intervention to raise human consciousness. Seeing impotence and hypocrisy everywhere, people generally feel less and less willing to align themselves spiritually. Yet, as we remain chaste to our traditions and willing to make sacrifices, we too can free others from the bondage of material existence while at the same time purchasing our own freedom.

Question: Is it really possible for us to take the place of another, assuming we have reached a level of selfless love? If it is possible, and we do exchange places with others who are suffering, is that not an intervention into their karmic patterns, which they were meant to live out for specific reasons?

Answer: The Supreme Lord does not want to see anyone suffering, what to speak of those who are most dear to him. Therefore, if a servant of the Lord who, out of selfless compassion, desires to change places with another, the Lord will intervene on his behalf as well as on behalf of the person whose suffering he wishes to alleviate.

Question: You spoke earlier about being willing to extend ourselves for our neighbor. In these modern times, however, it seems that "our neighbor" is a difficult term to define, as many professionals are currently part of a mass exodus from the urban center. Members of certain mosques and churches travel into the city for their particular service and then go back to suburbia, to live in what they consider a safer environment. Many spiritual organizations are now purchasing land to develop self-sufficiency and to escape the danger of the inner-city. My concern is that with so many talented individuals deserting a deteriorating situation, how do we as spiritualists continue to have an impact upon those who need us the most, even if they are no longer technically "our neighbors"?

Answer: Understand unequivocally that those persons and organizations who are exiting certain environments in order to save themselves will be part of the devastation. Understand that everything on this planet is highly monitored and people are aligned based on consciousness. Those who are merely concerned with self-preservation carry with them the consciousness of selfishness. Urban life itself is unnatural, filled with factories spewing pollution and a focus on superficial commodities. People feel boxed in because they have neither yards nor the ability to grow anything. However, those who are either trying to make adjustments to the city environment to facilitate better living for others, or those who are moving to more natural environments in order to demonstrate the possibility of simple living, high thinking show a more exalted consciousness. How can they not be recipients of divine protection?

A more natural environment allows us to commune well with the elemental. Living in the country facilitates connection with higher beings, too. While higher beings have always been coming to this particular planet—because at no time does God leave any of his parts and parcels alone—it is true that certain kinds of environments attract them. Natural environments, too, help us to be more aware of their presence. As people are frequently bombarded with massive air pollution, sound pollution, and lifestyle pollution in city environments, it is much more difficult for them to be sensitive to the presence of angels and messengers of God.

Striving to have a connection outside of the urban community is a good principle, in general. Those who have first-hand experience of war know that the cities are some of the worst environments in which to stay because people are packed together like rats in little cubby holes. Whatever happens in one street affects another street. Cities are frequently dangerous places, even in times of so-called peace. The situation for parents is particularly precarious: many live from day-to-day not knowing whether someone is going to snatch their child on the way to and from school, or whether their children are safe even while at school.

Nowadays, many people aspire to create not only environments that are physically secure, but those in which they can control the quality of food they eat, water they drink, and air they breathe. The increase in immune system problems in recent years is likely linked to the pollution of food and drinking water by toxic waste. Nuclear production and testing also contributes to the accumulation of toxic waste in the environment. Living closer to nature allows us to be less controlled by external situations, and simultaneously to access more of our inner nature. As we become healthier, we become more competent to share our knowledge with others. You cannot give what you do not have. You may have good intentions, but ultimately, if you are not strong internally, your actions will be sentimental. In order to really help people in these times, we must acquire a sufficient level of cognizance about modern adversarial forces in our society. A soldier who goes out with only good intentions is an easy target for devastation. We are under bombardment. We must know what positive action to take, as well as what negative situations to avoid as we march ahead.

Keep in mind that many souls will have to meet death as part of the cleansing affecting the planet. While some souls will have to be recycled, many souls will be able to remain here to create a heavenly atmosphere on earth. Souls with many pious credits have incarnated at this time in order to finish up some last homework before qualifying to go either to the heavenly kingdoms or to the spiritual worlds.

Question: Earlier you talked about receiving assistance from higher abodes. Are you indicating that as we lift our consciousness as a community and become more compassionate, then more help will be available to us?

Answer: Yes. Our future on the planet, individual and collective, is based ultimately on consciousness, which is monitored by agents of the Lord. It is interesting that most of the communes that have lasted internationally were started by a leader who was receptive to guidance from a higher being about the geographical location of the community, about what kind of practices to engage in, and about what sort of lifestyles to encourage. Those which came together merely as the result of good intentions later fell apart due to personality problems or a lack of solid infrastructure. Due to collective *karma* and connections from previous lives, certain souls come together to form communities. Due to consciousness, those in geographically safer environments may sometimes meet death faster than those living in a so-called risky area, while some souls who physically lose their bodies will be brought back to life. The prophet Isaiah, Lord Jesus, and certain demigods possess mystic powers to raise the dead. If we do the necessary in our physical environments, but ultimately depend on the Lord for the final outcome, we will attract great protection. We must do the needful, of course. It is foolish to think that we can just sit and meditate or retreat to the mountains or the bush and expect to be provided for.

We are both the recipients of mercy from various agents of the higher realms as well as targets of confusion and devastation from agents of the lower realms. Some souls have descended from the higher realms in order to raise the collective consciousness, and to lay the groundwork for a more harmonious and balanced environment. They easily attract those souls who are trying to be ethical, and who are aspiring to improve the conditions of others. The majority of souls on this planet are neutral: they can be influenced for good or evil depending on the dominant mindset permeating their surroundings. Due to these conditions, a massive subtle war is being waged as we speak between agents from both the higher and lower realms—a war to influence the environment, to win over as many personalities as possible. While most people attempt to live in environments which they consider safer according to their elementary knowledge of external factors, safety is determined by consciousness.

These are very delicate years in which people are being aligned according to different connections. Therefore, it is of crucial importance how we use our time, what kinds of places we visit, and what sorts of vibrations we choose to hear. It is especially important to keep focused. Many souls who have accumulated so many deposits in their spiritual bank accounts find themselves subject to heavy attack. Many spiritualists undergo a dark night of the soul during which they question the whole conception of a God. Some emerge with their faith intact, although institutions they depended upon no longer exist, or techniques they relied upon previously are simply not effective any more. Many souls can be lost if not guided properly. Wounded soldiers must receive reinforcements.

The armies of *māyā* are working overtime in these very critical periods to prevent as many people as possible from cashing in their pious credits. As you start leaving *māyā's* camp, a great effort is made to snatch you back. If you intend to seriously intensify your spiritual commitments, expect that your life will be struck by more incoherence. You will face great challenges, at least for a certain period, until you have stabilized yourself.

CHAPTER 4

The Language of Selflessness

Understanding Śrīla Prabhupāda's Instruction

Over thirty years ago, Śrīla Prabhupāda instructed me to be selfless, humble, and brave. It will take me the rest of this lifetime not only to understand but to fulfill his instructions properly. One way to arrive at a mature understanding of what selflessness, humility, and bravery truly mean is to intensify our appreciation of what Kṛṣṇa has given us.

Selflessness, on a mundane level, means thinking less of the self. Frequently viewed as the opposite of egocentricity, this sublime quality acquires deeper layers of meaning from a spiritual perspective. Real selflessness ironically means giving more attention to the self—that is, the real self, while at the same time putting aside the false self. As the real self or soul is pure, it is always involved in acts of compassion and devotion. The soul is *sac-cid-ānanda-vigrahaḥ*: eternal, full of knowledge, and enchanting bliss. Selflessness, as a word normally used in the English language, frequently implies negation of self, whereas spiritual selflessness means affirmation of the real self. I conceive of selflessness here as an act of self-purification and self-actualization. By sharing my introspection, I hope that it will act as a catalyst to assist you in examining personally whether you are either accessing selflessness or holding onto selfishness.

Are We Truly Selfless?

While materialists derive happiness from acquiring material things, pious people obtain the most enjoyment from helping others. Receiving appreciation for their deeds is part of what enlivens pious people, as well as knowing internally that they have done something wonderful. Rarely is a person in this world happy, even a pious person, when he or she helps another and does not receive approval. But for extraordinary souls, no external appreciation is needed. Whatever they do, they do for Kṛṣṇa. Let us be honest with ourselves. Which category do we fall into? Hopefully, none of us are like those who define the happiest moments of their lives by the acquisition of material possessions. Overjoyed when they finally buy a house or get a raise, materialists link happiness intimately to objects related to their own bodies or somebody else's body.

Pious people, on the other hand, are unsatisfied with just meditating on themselves. Situated somewhat in the mode of goodness, they strive to uplift others, but at the same time want to know that they are valued. The transcendental state surpasses piety, however, because it does not depend on recognition. Situated in the mode of pure goodness, true transcendentalists do not need external validation. Why should they depend on somebody else to let them know they have value, when they continually feel the approval of Kṛṣṇa within their hearts? Most of us, however, still seek happiness based on distinct reciprocation from others. If we do something we feel is wonderful, but do not receive the reciprocation we want, do we feel angry or disturbed, depressed or frustrated? If so, we are still trapped within the modes of material nature.

As spirit-souls, we desire to reach a point at which we experience God's presence powerfully in all things, in all circumstances, and at all times. In such a consciousness, we can genuinely work with and assist others, understanding sincerely that whatever we do then becomes an offering of great love to the Lord. Such a person will attain the highest level of happiness because very few obstacles will block them. Firstly, they will not allow themselves to be stopped by a lack of material possessions, as they operate outside the arena of the physical. Secondly, they will not be stagnated by pouring their emotional energy into expectations for external reciprocation, because whatever they undertake is for the benefit of the soul in connection with Kṛṣṇa. Therefore, they constantly find numerous opportunities for richer experiences of ever-deepening happiness.

Learning the Language of Selflessness

How important it is to truly reflect on ourselves! Let us go beyond just thinking of ourselves or others in a material sense. Let us surpass the need for external appreciation. We all want to connect with real love. We know theoretically that genuine love cannot be found outside of our connection with Kṛṣṇa. Yet, at the same time, most of us find it difficult to develop true selflessness, which is a prerequisite for experiencing real love.

Developing selflessness is like learning a new language. Most of us find it difficult to acquire new language skills, unless we are linguists by profession or possess a natural talent. Learning a new language means having to codify the world differently. It's quite a task to continue to interact in our normal environments, but to label the objects that surround us in a different way. Imagine that the words we usually use to describe a table or a chair, a man or a woman, belong to our previous language. Suddenly, we now have to use new vocabulary to describe familiar objects. Similarly, when trying to access selflessness, we do not have to change our environment or our activities, but we must transform the way we label and interact with them. Acknowledging that the false ego is part of our consciousness, we now need to question ourselves constantly about the source of our behavior. Ask yourself: Are my actions motivated by a desire for fame and adoration, or are they motivated by a longing to be fully present for another? Do my words stem from a hidden need to make the best arrangements for my own comfort, or do they come from a genuine desire to make the best connection with another person?

Taking Care of the Real Number One

Ironically, in this material existence we are forced to think that happiness means that we have to take care of ourselves—usually meaning the physical "me." *Māyā's* biggest trick is to bewilder us into believing that happiness lies in a day-to-day existence, focused around the satisfaction of our so-called needs. Such a mentality brings temporary stimulation amid an ocean of ongoing frustrations. Arranging for numerous illusions to distract those who want to be distracted, *māyā* creates a culture in which people are obsessed with capturing fleeting pleasures. If we choose to connect with transcendence, however, then we will experience consistent euphoria and ecstasy no matter what occurs in our immediate environment. One of the reasons great servants of the Lord genuinely do not mind going to the hellish planets or undertaking the most difficult tasks is the pleasure they derive from surrendering to the Lord. Realizing that remembering the Lord is everything, great devotees are only disturbed when something interferes with their ability to recall Him at every moment.

For materialists, life is so disappointing. Frequently, their greatest hope is to find a man or woman with whom to create a life. Because their suffering is frequently very intense, many people delude themselves into thinking that if they just find the right person, they can create their own universe with him or her, shutting off the harsh external world. This concept is merely sentimental as in most cases an individual has to interact with so many other persons. The one person they choose as a partner is essentially an amalgamation of past and present experiences and influences. It is impossible to create the self-contained association about which many of us dream. Even if we think we have found the perfect partner, the marriage will be a failure if we expect to derive our entire sense of security and contentment from each other. Men and women cannot give each other everything. Some experiences and perceptions men have to get from other men, and women from other women, ones which they can bring back and use to enrich their primary partnership.

Whether married or single, the more we access selflessness, the more joyful we will become. Without a doubt, the happiest people I have ever known are the most selfless. The happiest times in my own life were when I acted with a sincere desire to become selfless. When people center their entire existence on what they can gain for themselves, they frequently end up frustrated and bored. Notice how intensely you suffer when you keep trying to arrange the world for your own pleasures. Even though we may be able to manipulate many variables, ultimately we end up disappointed because this activity does not touch the deepest core of our existence.

If asked whether they derive most of their happiness from material objects, most devotees will honestly say no. The majority of us may still be on the level at which, yes, our happiness comes from serving those we care about and from situations in which we feel distinct appreciation. The sense of well-being, and occasionally euphoria, which accompanies our service will then come and go. Do we not wish to come to a point at which happiness does not fluctuate but remains consistent? While the sense of well-being we derive in this state of consciousness is sometimes in the forefront, and sometimes in the background, Kṛṣṇa's reciprocation is always dependable. The more we serve others as a service to Kṛṣṇa, the more consistent will be the reciprocation we crave. Unlike conditioned souls, Kṛṣṇa is always available to reciprocate with us, and is ever-willing to send us opportunities to connect with Him more deeply. Let us try to access a joy both deeper and more enduring than anything we have ever experienced by developing selflessness in connection with the Lord.

Anxiety and Low Self-Esteem Block Selflessness

Being Selfless Is a Difficult Instruction was the working title of *Meditation 6* from *The Beggar III*, which we subsequently published as *Think More of Others and Less of Yourself.* Here, I reflect upon Śrīla Prabhupāda's instruction in a small attempt to make his words as integral a part of my existence as breathing. Selected passages from *Meditation 6* follow, together with some realizations I hope you will find helpful in developing the sublime quality of selflessness.

> *My dear spiritual master, over the years in my service to you, one of the most difficult instructions you gave me was for me to be selfless. Normally when I think of*

being selfless, anxiety flares up in my heart and mind. The thought naturally arouses emotions of fear, for I can't help feeling that this means giving up my entire identity—all my needs and aspirations. It sounds like you're instructing me to become a doormat for others' desires, and to become a non-entity.

When you instruct me this way, my false ego screams: "No way! That is total insanity!" Thank you so much for showing me by your lifestyle that being selfless does not mean giving up my identity, but reclaiming my pure and royal identity. It does not mean I must give up my needs, but I must replace my desires with the actual, pure needs that are eternally attached to my soul.

My spiritual master spoke, "Selflessness does not mean to give up pursuing adventurous goals, but rather to attach ourselves to transcendental goals. Actual selflessness means we must genuinely access humility and submissiveness. This can be very scary, because we normally identify humility and submissiveness with low self-esteem.

"Low self-esteem can cause people to give up their identity and their ability to explore, create, and achieve, while letting others control their thoughts and actions. But this is never the result of genuine selflessness. Genuine selflessness is an empowering process that grants us more and more autonomy."

I pondered my master's words and then revealed more of my apprehensions, "My dear spiritual master, one of the most difficult instructions you've given me is to be selfless. I want to obey this order, but doesn't being selfless mean that I will eventually grow bored and lazy, for I will always be absorbed in helping to serve and facilitate others? Doesn't being selfless mean I will never experience satisfaction?"

Why Am I Bored?

Truly becoming selfless automatically negates boredom and laziness, as once we stop focusing solely on our own concerns, we find there are so many things to do! So many people are suffering; so many problems need to be solved. Seize the chance to facilitate and see what you can do. There is no question of either boredom or laziness. Being bored indicates a lack of a sense of adventure, a reluctance to rise to a challenge. Just look at your own community. What can you do to improve it? If we remain locked into selfish reflections, then boredom and laziness will undoubtedly set in as we fail to capitalize on the chance to be there for someone else. So-called problems and setbacks are golden opportunities to glorify our *guru* more, to serve him or her better and, most of all, to work on ourselves so that we can become better representatives of *bhakti*. When we feel bored, we should know that this feeling is a red flag signifying that something is awry in our consciousness. Ask yourself, "Am I bored because I am not using my time wisely? Could it be that I'm fed up most of the time because I'm too selfish?"

Boredom indicates an unhealthy obsession with what we think we should be experiencing. If boredom is a familiar part of our day-to-day exchanges, then we should know that we are pouring too much energy into our self-centered material desires, plans, ideas, and frustrations. We cannot come to Kṛṣṇa with selfishness. Are we really prepared to plunge deeply into our consciousness to weed out rationalizations which prevent us from surrendering to Kṛṣṇa?

Dissatisfaction Indicates Selfishness

This time I decided to write to my mentor. "My dear spiritual master," I wrote, "one of the most difficult instructions you gave me was to be selfless. I normally look at all kinds of sights for my enjoyment. My ears are very active in trying to hear something for their enjoyment. And my nose, mouth, and stomach never take a vacation from searching for more material enjoyment. My genitals also never retire from anticipating illicit activity.

"I can understand that if I were truly selfless, none of these pulls from my senses would be a problem, for I would not allow my mind to give into the harassments of the environment, or into my egocentric desires."

The *vegas*, or pushings of the senses, are all deeply connected with desire for self-stimulation and pleasure. As we become more and more selfless, we will naturally experience less agitation due to our successful endeavor to remove ourselves from the center of our personal universe. When we stop placing top priority on our physical needs, we can address the real self, which does not need anything material to experience happiness. To what degree are we experiencing mental agitation, food cravings, and sexual anxieties? The dominance of these disturbances in our lives is concomitant with our selfishness.

Most of us are attuned to satisfying needs that are separate from our connection with the Lord. Know that when we are properly connected to Kṛṣṇa, all our needs will be satisfied in full. Those rare souls who have renounced pride do not feel a lacking in their lives. On the contrary, releasing pride creates a space within their consciousness to receive greater blessings. Most of us have experienced denying ourselves immediate gratification in order to attain a higher goal. Even though we inconvenienced ourselves in certain ways, we found that being distracted from our own particular issues invites a certain happiness and satisfaction. When we are being less self-centered, a natural solace arises—how much more so when our activity is connected with Kṛṣṇa.

The senses will be very much at rest when they are focused on Kṛṣṇa. Notice that when you feel less Kṛṣṇa conscious, you want to eat more, sleep more, and are more sexually agitated. These urges indicate that you have placed Kṛṣṇa's plan on the back-burner. Perhaps you have detected that when you are not thinking of facilitating the devotees or your family based on a spiritual connection, then the environment suddenly seems to pounce. Suddenly, we find ourselves so disturbed by our senses. These discomforts are red flags which indicate that we have to work more intensely on becoming genuinely selfless.

"My dear spiritual master," I wrote in another letter, "one of the most difficult instructions you gave me was to be selfless. I am so covered with jealousy and envy. But if I were truly selfless I would be so happy to see others excel and achieve. My real happiness would not be in my own accomplishments but in the success of others.

"I would feel their sadness, pain and failures, as well as their happiness, joy, and success. Until this is a spontaneous and natural reaction, I know that I am far from being selfless. I am still absorbed in so many fears coming from all my senses, mind, and even intelligence. If I want to become truly selfless, I realize that I must see, smell, hear, taste, speak, feel, and do only those things that I know would be pleasing to you."

Jealousy is only associated with self-centered concerns. Selflessness cancels out jealousy. Those in the higher heavenly planets like Brahmaloka do not feel misery or pain, except when they think of others who are suffering in the lower planetary systems. They do not experience misery on their own account, as they have advanced to the stage at which they are focused on divinity and on associating with others in a godly way.

"Actually, anytime I think that I am the enjoyer, I am destined to experience fears and agitations. And every time I experience such disturbances, I must see it as another sign of selfishness.

"By your mercy, my dear spiritual guide, I can better understand that genuine selflessness is not about thinking less of myself, it's thinking of myself less."

Normally we think of ourselves constantly, but in so many improper ways. Thinking of oneself less means minimizing improper reflections and considerations.

We Are Only Caretakers

I wrote letters for months… "My dear spiritual master, one of the most difficult instructions you gave me was to become selfless. If I took this seriously I would take care of all the things and people under my jurisdiction, and I would treat all of my possessions with utmost care. I would never be incompetent, impersonal, insensitive, or neglectful, for I would realize that everything belongs to God and must be offered back to Him in such a way that the real Owner would be pleased. All that we consider ours has come to us by Kṛṣṇa's mercy and will one day be taken away, therefore we are only caretakers."

We notice that Śrīla Prabhupāda was not only careful with spiritual paraphernalia, but also treated even mundane objects with care. Often, we hear that during his morning walks, Śrīla Prabhupāda would stop to turn off a running faucet. Being Kṛṣṇa conscious means seeing everything as existing for Kṛṣṇa's use. Therefore, we must take good care of our facilities, whether they are cars, buildings, or houses, as well as those entrusted to our care like family members, cows, or pets.

If we realize that everything belongs to God, we will maneuver the material energy in an enchanting way in order to offer it back to Him. But if we see ourselves as proprietors, then how can we make such an offering? If we see the temporary products of this world as our own, then we miss the opportunity to be Kṛṣṇa conscious. Being Kṛṣṇa conscious means thinking of the Lord at all times, in all circumstances. We are only the caretakers. Let that be your constant meditation. Everything we have will dissolve at some point, because everything material is temporary. What we take from one lifetime to another is not material commodities, but the consciousness associated with them. Each time we leave these bodies, we take with us reactions resulting from our past interactions with matter.

"The fact that I am often incompetent, impersonal, insensitive, and neglectful confirms that I am selfish and overly possessive. I am not properly recognizing who the real Owner is or how I should treat His possessions. By your mercy, my dear spiritual guide, I can further understand that genuine selflessness is not about thinking less of myself, it's thinking of myself less.

"My dear spiritual master, one of the most difficult instructions you gave me was to be selfless. If I had more gratitude, and more importantly if I did not minimize and doubt your and Kṛṣṇa's mercy, I would surely be a more loving and selfless servant!"

Our selfishness is sometimes fed by our doubts and our fears. When we doubt the Lord's mercy, we are querying His protection. Who of us does not secretly fear that if we make ourselves more available, if we try to surrender more, and if are better servants, then our material demands will not be met? Let us remind ourselves, however, that the material energy is controlled by the Lord. Truly, who will facilitate us better than the Supreme?

Selflessness Means Divine Strength

"You have been so kind to help me understand how I minimize your mercy. My selfish attachments and perceptions have caused me to hold onto low self-esteem or pride, pursuits of sense gratification, fears and jealousy, enviousness, incompetence, impersonalism, insensitivity, neglectfulness, doubts, and lack of gratitude.

"By your mercy, I now clearly understand that genuine selflessness is not about thinking less of myself, it's thinking of myself less. But I admit that I am perplexed. Why has this been such a difficult instruction for me to follow?"

My spiritual master replied, "Yes my beloved, not only will this continue to be a most difficult instruction to honor, but it will be impossible for you to fully honor as long as you are convinced you can do it on your own strength. But, as you more genuinely accept my grace and mercy, you will receive even more empowerment to rise above these remaining blocks."

"Beloved," my mentor continued, "it is actually far simpler than you think. Simply continue thinking of yourself less and your whole existence will become more infused with the glorious, sublime mercy of our worshipful Lord and His Divine Consort."

The dominant culture of sense gratification has a major impact on practically everyone's consciousness. It is a fact that avoiding temptations, what to say of steering clear of sinful reflections, can be very difficult when most of us are constantly surrounded by stimuli in the environment which urge us to enjoy life at any cost. Simply attempting to live a moral life places us in the minority. How can we possibly hope to rise above it on our own? We can conquer over the influences of materialism only with the help of healthy association, together with the mercy of the Lord. Ultimately, no temptation is greater than Kṛṣṇa. If we genuinely turn to the Lord, then we will find that the boredom, the frustration, and the setbacks that are aligned with selfishness will dissolve. Simultaneously, we will discover many more opportunities to try to be love-in-action, to attempt to love our brother or sister even more than ourselves.

Let us try harder to claim our natural birthright. Rather than being stagnated by temporary setbacks, or overwhelmed by temptation, let us attend to our own genuine needs. Our needs are similar to those of others, because we all share a common humanity, a deep craving to reconnect at a more intense level with the Godhead. While we cannot be permanently satisfied by different material stimulations, the soul becomes everlastingly fulfilled as we embark on rediscovering our true identity as eternal spiritual beings. Feelings that our lives are incomplete, or experiencing boredom and frustration despite so many opportunities for growth, are not due to Kṛṣṇa or Śrīla Prabhupāda, but rather due to our lack of desire to plunge deeper into devotional service. Similarly, anytime we experience anxiety, laziness, or jealousy, we should know that those negative emotions do not emanate from a platform of purity, compassion, love or selflessness, but stem directly from personal desires for distinction, adoration, and various types of profit.

It is not possible to be selfless without being meek and humble. And genuine humility means strength—strength to keep striving for truth, strength to keep accessing compassion, strength to keep looking for deeper love, and strength to be ready to reciprocate.

As Lord Kṛṣṇa advises Arjuna in *Bhagavad-gītā* 3.43:

evaṁ buddheḥ paraṁ buddhvā
saṁstabhyātmānam ātmanā
jahi śatruṁ mahā-bāho
kāma-rūpaṁ durāsadam

> Thus knowing oneself to be transcendental to the material senses, mind and intelligence, O mighty-armed Arjuna, one should steady the mind by deliberate spiritual intelligence [Kṛṣṇa consciousness] and thus—by spiritual strength—conquer this insatiable enemy known as lust.

Being Brave

Why did Śrīla Prabhupāda mention bravery to me? Śrīla Prabhupāda's first name, Abhaya, epitomized fearlessness. Like all true saints, he was never eager to be a part of normalcy. Great personalities do not merely go along with whatever is comfortable, but they are literally spiritual revolutionaries. Not that one should be foolishly brave, but after checking in with *guru*, *sādhu*, and *śāstra*, one should launch ahead with great zeal and boldness. One is fearlessly eager because one feels lovingly protected and guided. One is ready to respond enthusiastically to the call of duty.

If we are not selfless or humble, what is the question of being transcendentally brave? As I write at the end of *Meditation 7: Being Selfless, Humble, and Brave* from the *Beggar III*:

> *Unless one is truly selfless and humble, one will not value others sufficiently and will therefore mainly act for his or her own so-called welfare. Where there is proper selflessness and humility, a devotee will eagerly become the servant of others. A selfless, humble devotee is so brave that if necessary, he or she will stand alone to defend truth and integrity, despite being in the minority.*
>
> *The brave devotee is determined to represent the ācāryas with his or her best offerings to them. A brave devotee is the finest spiritual warrior because he fights on the subtle battlefield of consciousness with weapons of compassion, truth and love. A brave devotee monitors his actions and is guided by guru, sādhu and śāstra. Thus, he or she proceeds with great confidence and competence.*
>
> *It is obvious that I will die soon, and when I look at my present status, I realize I am lacking in three of the most important Vaiṣṇava qualities. I am not sufficiently humble, selfless or brave, and there is hardly sufficient time to transform my character. I have already wasted*

so many years by being ungrateful and lamenting. My obstacles are very clear to me now. I must become truly selfless, humble and brave. But even knowing what I must develop and work on doesn't diminish the task, for my false ego also knows this and it has designed many means to destroy my attempts.

How will I be able to fully help myself surrender when I am my own greatest enemy? I have only a little time left to become selfless, humble and brave, but my false ego laughs and accuses, "It is already too late, you failure. Just look at how many times you've tried and failed before."

But maybe it is not too late. Perhaps, Beloved, you can help me this time.

Question: How was it possible for our previous *ācāryas* to maintain such a high level of consciousness at every moment?

Answer: For the pure servants of God, it is always sublimely easy to express their love and receive love in a selfless way, as our unnatural conditioning of selfishness is not part of their mentality. The nature of the soul is purely selfless, purely rapt with love and devotion. As we reclaim our natural status, we will not find it problematic to be selfless, as it is an inherent part of our constitution. We are made in the image of God, but somehow we have become addicted to the material energy.

Just like an alcoholic who finds it very difficult to refuse a drink, whether she is alone or in a crowd, so too do we find it takes a lot of energy to refuse to participate in the material paradigm. Someone who is not an alcoholic, however, does not find drinking a temptation. Similarly, the pure servants of the Lord are not controlled by unhealthy paradigms. They actually have no desire to participate in them. Addicts are sometimes perplexed by those who are not seduced by their drug of choice, not understanding how it's not an integral part of their life space. Those who cherish healthy lifestyles generally find the thought of taking drugs abhorrent. For them, it's an activity that exists outside of their consciousness, outside of their appetites and desires. We have become so acculturated to functioning in a selfish mindset that it has become an integral part of us, just as the craving for alcohol or drugs is an inseparable part of an addict's existence. However, just as there was once a time when an alcoholic or drug addict had yet to conceive of getting drunk or high, so too were we once free of addiction to material nature.

Question: You mentioned that we can't become selfless on our own strength, and that we need to open ourselves up to receive the grace of *guru*. At the same time, you emphasized that we must endeavor to become selfless. How do we balance both instructions?

Answer: It is almost impossible for a prisoner whose hands are tied to escape by himself. But if someone comes and helps to sever the chains, then the prisoner has a stronger possibility of attaining freedom. In the same way, the Lord is always arranging help for the imprisoned living entity, but so often we deny or minimize His helping hand. God never places us into situations which do not allow us to know Him, to connect with His mercy, or to become freed from sin. Never. If that were the case, it would mean that sin is as strong or stronger than the Supreme. It would mean that the

Lord is not at all merciful, that He intentionally places us in situations which are beyond our ability to transcend.

Becoming free is intimately connected with genuinely recognizing one's condition and genuinely wanting help. Neophyte devotees can be likened to sick people who are trying different types of healing modalities. In many cases, we go from one procedure to the next without properly following the regimen. We get the prescription, maybe even purchase the medicine, but do not take it. We go from allopathic treatment, to homeopathic, from acupuncture to acupressure, but do not really take advantage of any treatment properly. At the same time, the sick person has a desire to be healed. Or rather, there is enough desire to seek help, but not enough to follow through with the treatment. Similarly, in spiritual life, sometimes we have good intentions about trying to be more devotional, but they do not penetrate our consciousness to a deep level. Due to lack of deep desire on our part, we find that we heal partially, but not completely. Just like the ambivalent patient who seeks medical help but cannot give up some unhealthy habits, we adhere tightly to attachments which are detrimental for spiritual advancement.

If, as patients, we place ourselves solely under the doctor's care, we stand a much greater chance of complete recovery. By presenting ourselves at the mercy of the Lord more and more, we gain the strength to overcome any kind of adversity. Mercy will undoubtedly come when we invite it. But we must take care not to block it at the same time. Becoming selfless is difficult, but it is not impossible. It is difficult on our own because we have placed ourselves in a difficult situation by our own intelligence.

Therefore, our intelligence itself is deviant. It has kept us attracted and attached to many harmful patterns lifetime after lifetime. Normally, we would be suspicious of someone who has been tricking us our whole life and all of a sudden wants to become our best friend. When we come to spiritual life, the mind and intelligence play all kinds of tricks which cause us to rationalize so many things. Frequently, those who are the most intelligent find the greatest ways to rationalize their deviations. We want to spiritualize the intelligence and the mind. Spiritualizing means letting more of the God-factor in. Our mind is often more of an enemy than a friend, because it's been conditioned to respond to the senses, and the senses are conditioned mainly to respond to the environment. If we just let the mind have its day, then we should expect trouble.

The mind will tell us, "I don't think it's healthy for you to be too selfless. After all, you need a life. You deserve to feel good. Just be happy that misfortunes happened to somebody else today and not to you. Don't worry about someone else's impoverishment or problem or setback, because that is life. Just be thankful you did not have to endure it!" We must examine our minds closely, and allow spiritual absorption to rectify them.

Contemplate the fact that at every moment, we are presented with amazing opportunities to deepen our relationship with Kṛṣṇa. Not a day goes by when the opportunity does not present itself. Remember that it's not the real pure ego, but rather the false ego that interferes with our ability to receive God's love, compassion, and protection. Feeling lazy, bored, sexually agitated, wasteful, or ungrateful are subtle red flags alerting us that we are too focused on our false selves. In these states of consciousness, we are too self-centered to be effective agents of divinity.

Beloved, always remind yourself that the more you are selfless and compassionate, the more everyday will become an exciting adventure. Seize the chance to try to help another, seize the chance to improve the quality of your character. We can always be more grateful for the amazing opportunities the Lord constantly arranges for us.

Chapter 5

When We Wound the Spiritual Master

Refusal to Surrender Blocks the Paramparā

Many of us had heard about the process of surrender within the first few days of coming in contact with devotees, but we all need to remind one another constantly of how to surrender, why we are surrendering, why we want to fall back into the arms of the Lord. Therefore, we must remind each other to cleanse ourselves by abstaining from gross sinful activities and by observing the four regulative principles. But the principles are merely the beginning. Now we must sever ourselves from the subtle attachments and weeds. Kṛṣṇa cannot be bribed. Aware of how we handle the gross elements, Kṛṣṇa is primarily concerned with whether or not we allow miracles to take place. We are connected to Him like the little sparrow that goes to the ocean and tries to futilely drink up the water on her own—but then Garuḍa comes. That is our opposition—the ocean. To invoke intense devotion by our desire to see changes in a very difficult environment, despite the forces of negativity that surround us—this is what Kṛṣṇa wants from us. We are to feel that Kṛṣṇa will protect us in any situation.

Kṛṣṇa wants to see that we are so desirous to make a proper offering to Śrīla Prabhupāda that we allow ourselves to become empowered far beyond our own abilities.

Our own abilities will never be enough, because what we have to offer Śrīla Prabhupāda will never be enough—unless we offer back to him as he desires. We are either involved in helping Śrīla Prabhupāda on his mission, or else we are literally involved in attacking the *paramparā* system, the disciplic succession of Vaiṣṇava saints. As the mind begins to engage in the fear associated with the intoxication of sense gratification, so do the demons progress in their strategy.

What is real violence? Violence occurs when we involve ourselves in any activity which constitutes a distraction to the devotional process. Violence occurs when we associate with one another in ways which reinforce a negative subculture. Violence occurs when we reduce Kṛṣṇa consciousness to the level of an ordinary religion rather than honoring it as a lifestyle, a commitment, and an intensely wonderful experience. Every time we minimize chanting our rounds, every time we avoid reading the scriptures, every time we skip classes, or every time we ignore a chance to preach, we are wounding Śrīla Prabhupāda.

Imagine Śrīla Prabhupāda is coming up the steps to your house or *āśrama*. Imagine he is carrying many packages. Is it not the duty of all of us to assume some of that burden and to move up the steps with him, joyfully and carefully? Is it not destructive if we simply brush past him, or if we add more heavy parcels for him to lift? What if we are literally bringing obstacles into his path, so that he may trip? Engaging in activities that are outside the royal path of devotion attracts obstacles that cause stagnation and confusion. Śrīla Prabhupāda gave us such simple principles: books are the basis, preaching is the essence, utility is the principle, and purity is the force. Our duty is to read the books, to understand the spiritual rule of law, and to put it into practice. Use the books as a window to the spiritual world. Take the philosophy off the theoretical level and apply it. Our greatest preaching happens by our own examples.

A preacher must use strategy because we are on a battlefield. We are all fighting our own Battle of Kurukṣetra. As ordinary weaponry is not sufficient, our strategy must invoke divine intervention. However, nothing significant can occur without purity. Without purity we will just engage in various permutations of the material energy, and quickly become frustrated. The demons attack in two major ways: first they weaken one to sense gratification and then they frustrate one to such an extent that one loses enthusiasm to stay involved in spiritual warfare in the community of Vaiṣṇavas. We cannot continue without stimulation. If we are not feeling stimulated from the spiritual connection, then we find ourselves turning back to sense gratification. Many great generals in our movement have become frustrated due to identification with material nature, or with the material result. Feeling a void, they attempt to fill that void with sense gratification. Not allowing Kṛṣṇa to come through sufficiently, they ultimately engage in activities that wound Śrīla Prabhupāda.

Spiritual versus Material Weaponry

We are to use spiritual strategy to counteract material weaponry. We do not use the same techniques employed by the enemy, who has been tremendously competent in using them since time immemorial, and then think we will be successful. Know that if we lack sufficient knowledge of the enemy's field of activity, then we are incomplete. We have to understand *pravṛtti* and *nivṛtti*, positive and negative action: to be able to assess what is to be done, and also what not to do. In warfare, it is never sufficient merely to possess weapons without understanding the adversary. In such circumstances, we may use the weapons in the wrong way, or not feel the necessity to use them when we should.

Let us look at our own lives. Consider that just as Kṛṣṇa has no favorites, *māyā* has no favorites either. We all possess a bank account that categorically accumulates our devotional credits and also extracts our debits. Sometimes, we keep debiting, coasting somewhat on previous deposits. But, like money in the bank, our credit balance can only last so long. We have to keep replenishing and recharging ourselves through the culture of devotion. Otherwise as the trance of *māyā* increases, we may find ourselves overwhelmed. Failing to muster a strong resistance, we realize too late that our resources are dangerously depleted.

Śrīla Prabhupāda came to show us how to sleep, how to eat, how to interact, and how to make every single aspect of our lives perfect. Until very recently, we were residents of the material world caught up in the material paradigm. Therefore, a total change of perspective is necessary. If we now want to pursue the spiritual world, we must tune into how people talk in the spiritual world, how they deal with conflicts, how they are unaffected by happiness and distress, and how they use every situation to glorify the Lord to a greater degree. And as we do so, how can Kṛṣṇa not give us increasing opportunities to glorify Him?

Śrīla Prabhupāda designed an ingenious system to heal the whole planet. He has given us a strategy to literally attract the heavens and flood the world with spiritual culture. We therefore have a great responsibility. As our father, grandfather, or great-grandfather, Śrīla Prabhupāda will want to know, "What did you do with my gift?" And we may say, "I could've done this, but my temple commander, but my president, but my GBC, but my *guru*...," but he wants to know, "What did you do for my service?" Yes, all of the problems are there. Obstacles are designed to be a part of our field of activities to test us, to enable us to triumph ultimately despite such impediments.

Remember that Mahārāja Ambarīṣa was also put into great difficulty. Although Mahārāja Ambarīṣa followed the correct śāstric procedure in receiving honored guests, Durvāsā Muni nevertheless became unreasonably angry with him. Pulling his hair out in rage, the Muni produced a fire demon to kill the king. But Mahārāja Ambarīṣa remained fixed to serve. Due to his proper devotion, dedication, attentiveness and faith, the Lord personally arranged for Ambarīṣa Mahārāja's protection through His Sudarśana *cakra*. A fiery weapon which annihilated the demon immediately, the *cakra* chased Durvāsā Muni throughout the three worlds until he surrendered at the feet of the humble king.

Mahārāja Ambarīṣa was not just a simple *sādhu*. He was involved in many manipulations of the material energy, yet Kṛṣṇa came through because the king never forgot who he was doing it for and how he was to do it. Mahārāja Ambarīṣa gave more and more strength to the *paramparā* system. As we allow people to engage in impersonalism and materialism, as we let them accept those philosophies as the all in all, so too do we sabotage the *paramparā* system. We are accountable to Śrīla Mādhavendra Purī, Śrīla Bhaktivinoda Ṭhākura, and all the venerable saints in our line. Yes, we have accountability. How can we become loyal and faithful without the mercy of these great representatives? And how can we attain their mercy if we do not move aside to let the mercy come through?

Ambiguity Is Māyā

God's love is always available and accessible. It has been since time immemorial. God's love has never changed and never will change, just as the process to attain that supreme love has stayed the same. Love brings love. Devotion brings more devotion just as violence brings violence. Anger brings anger. And lust ignites, becomes infectious, and brings disaster. The material world is a complete attack on basic human existence. At this point in time, the instruments of communication appear to have reached new heights. But intelligibility is at a low. By intelligibility, I mean the real ability of people to communicate, to understand one other, and to perceive the goal of life. Therefore, there is a dire need to remove many unnecessary obstacles that cause us to miss connections with God's love.

Surrender opens the door to love. In the process of surrender, we are to accept that which is favorable and to reject that which is unfavorable. But in great times of complexities, what is to be considered unfavorable? Modern thought says, "I have my truth, she has her truth, they have their truths." This type of thinking is demoniac, based on transitory considerations and ambiguities. Ambiguity is *māyā* because ambiguity opens the door for more ambivalence to come through. Kṛṣṇa does not come through very easily when we have not made a proper seat available for Him by the cleansing of our minds and hearts.

Understand that Kṛṣṇa consciousness is not a rational process. It is far beyond rationality. As aspiring devotees, we engage in activities that are diametrically opposed to material existence. We strive hard to be selfless and humble, not claiming proprietorship. We try with all our might to break free of *ahaṅkāra*, which bases its success on how much it is ingratiated. We are literally at war with the material universe. This war manifests mainly through battles within our own minds. Our greatest patterns of conditioning are within the mind. So how do we recondition ourselves? By looking at those who are not conditioned. We study examples of exemplary Vaiṣṇava behavior such as that of Mahārāja Ambarīṣa, the grandson of Vaivasvata Manu. As emperor of the entire planet, Mahārāja Ambarīṣa's range of jurisdiction was phenomenal. A tremendous administrator, Mahārāja Ambarīṣa was so humble that he claimed not a single blade of grass as his own. Due to his intense level of surrender, Mahārāja Ambarīṣa became a puppet for Kṛṣṇa's use. Similarly, in our process of surrender, we must remind ourselves always to depend on the mercy of Kṛṣṇa.

While mercy is always present, dependence is very awkward without faith. Dependence becomes difficult if we feel no need to depend. Behaving independently, we become prime candidates for attack. We do not realize how dangerous it is to be in the material body, how precarious it is at this time in world history to be a spiritualist, when demons are primarily in charge of the planet. Demons clearly understand where devotion is blossoming and who the devotees are. Because the material world is the abode of Durgā, it is the environment of abuse. We are visitors in a foreign environment. Therefore, we are very much at the mercy of the situation unless we take shelter of a force beyond planetary *karma*. This planet is practically dying. As a living entity, she is being abused on all levels. And here we are, somehow trying to be spiritual in a totally material environment. We must use the material, as it is *śakti*, part of Kṛṣṇa's energies. We are not to misuse Kṛṣṇa's *śakti* or deny it, but we are to employ material facilities in such a way that shows we are being responsible to the one who really owns it—Kṛṣṇa.

Anti-Material Strategies

In *Bhagavad-gītā* 9.31, Śrī Kṛṣṇa promises Arjuna:

> *kṣipraṁ bhavati dharmātmā*
> *śaśvac-chāntiṁ nigacchati*
> *kaunteya pratijānīhi*
> *na me bhaktaḥ praṇaśyati*

> He quickly becomes righteous and attains lasting peace. O son of Kuntī, declare it boldly that My devotee never perishes.

Kṛṣṇa promises to save us. Yet His promise does not mean that we will not have to struggle with the material energy. While confrontation with the modes is ever-present, it should not become a serious obstacle. One who is dear to Kṛṣṇa is unaffected by the three modes of material nature. We should strive to connect increasingly with the anti-material, with the spiritual family. What we do with what Kṛṣṇa makes available for us determines our spiritual future. We have to assess our priorities carefully, as they determine how much we allow Kṛṣṇa to come through. Our priorities also control the extent to which we use what belongs to Kṛṣṇa and then claim proprietorship. To what extent are we enjoying and using? To what extent are we preparing ourselves for residence in the heavenly kingdoms, at best? Again, we must come in and out of this *martya-loka*. We are foreigners in a hellish environment that daily becomes more and more hellish. Intense devotion means the ability to sustain wounds for our *guru*. That is the quality of devotion with which the soul yearns to connect—devotion which brings unlimited realizations and boundless pleasures, beyond anything experienced in the material realm. To achieve an intense level of *bhakti*, we need to immerse ourselves in anti-material thinking and activities.

Let us return again to the exemplary behavior of Mahārāja Ambarīṣa. When attacked, the king did not attempt to defend himself by ordinary methods, but faced his assailant with the power of transcendental love. Therefore, Mahārāja Ambarīṣa could not be attacked, even by a powerful *yogī* like Durvāsā Muni, who had acquired all the *siddhis*, or mystic powers, but who ultimately failed to defeat a great servant of the Lord. Śrīla Prabhupāda gave us his unalloyed love. Most of us did many things we would never have done for anyone, due to his love. It is therefore our duty not to wound him, but to capture some of that love and distribute it. By distributing his love with zeal, we activate a tremendously powerful weapon in these times of great anxiety and gloom which permeate this particular planet.

In order to distribute Śrīla Prabhupāda's unalloyed love, we must engage in a cleansing of the heart similar in quality to the thorough cleaning of the Guṇḍicā temple undertaken by Lord Caitanya in Jagannātha Purī. Before Lord Jagannātha, Baladeva, and Subhadrā left the Jagannātha Mandira to reside in the Guṇḍicā temple for eight days during the annual Rathayātrā festival, Mahāprabhu personally led hundreds of devotees in sanctifying the place. Once the devotees had cleaned the temple of dust and straw, Mahāprabhu encouraged them to clean it again, to remove the subtle dirt. Subtle dirt is comparable to subtle *anarthas*, which bring higher opposition and do not allow the deeper levels of devotion to take place. Duplicity and faultfinding are part of the abode of Durgā. We must be actively involved in searching out *māyā*. We remove *māyā* by love-finding instead of faultfinding. At the same time, we are not ostriches. We do not put our heads in the sand. We do the opposite; we search and see where we can inject the love, knowing that love acts as a light to destroy the nescience. We do not go into darkness with more darkness, ready to engage in combat.

How do we avoid duplicity? We make many mistakes. The administrators make many mistakes but those under us should know that we love and we care about them. Because we are acting in their best interests, that mistake will not cause them devastation. In fact, the mistake or the difficulty simply increases devotion because it brings up a need to address an issue with a sense of caring. Desire for fame and high position is a serious weed that has to be uprooted. Are we willing to engage in a service continuously if it brings no adoration? Are we ready to offer our lives? I want to learn from my godbrothers how to be an agent for transcendental love, knowing that my life is at stake. I want to learn from them how to live as a devotee who understands the difficulties and yet is still able to give eagerly, despite the odds. Even after being mortally wounded, a genuine devotee's faith increases, not decreases. That is transcendental—to transcend, to go beyond the norms.

ISKCON Comes from the Spiritual World

In *Bhagavad-gītā* 12.20, Śrī Kṛṣṇa confides in Arjuna:

ye tu dharmāmṛtam idaṁ
yathoktaṁ paryupāsate
śraddadhānā mat-paramā
bhaktās te 'tīva me priyāḥ

> Those who follow this imperishable path of devotional service and who completely engage themselves with faith, making Me the supreme goal, are very, very dear to Me.

One who is dear to Lord Kṛṣṇa is not relegated by ordinary considerations. ISKCON is not an ordinary movement. These scriptures are arrangements from the spiritual world. They contain recipes and formulas for spiritual success. These scriptures have been activated by *nitya-siddhas*, eternally liberated associates of the Lord, who come down to these hells just to show us that God's love is accessible. They have not come down to give a performance. If they were simply acting as pure devotees, we would see them as madmen. But they tone themselves down in order to demonstrate personally what we are supposed to do, how we are supposed to think, and how we are supposed to interact with one other.

Nitya-siddhas embody ever-increasing devotion. If our devotion does not increase, we will become casualties. The quality of devotion we attained five or ten years ago, or even two years ago, is not sufficient. *Māyā* has become more powerful. Her attacks are more devastating. Therefore, we have to access greater strength and a higher level of acceleration to defend ourselves properly, to conquer the obstacles. If the quality of our devotion has decreased rather than increased, then we may as well lay ourselves out in the open to be sacrificed. So as we strengthen our weaponry, we remind and inspire one another, and go out to battle as a full-force brigade. As a unified, armed brigade, we can engage in successful spiritual warfare.

As we make the proper connections, we find they will pull us through many impediments. If we do not, we will encounter obstacles with which we will identify, and therefore waste time in unnecessary exertion of energies. There are many subtle *aparādhas* to avoid: *nāma-aparādha*, offenses against the Holy Name; *dhāma-aparādha*, offenses against the holy places; *sevā-aparādha*, offenses committed during service to the deity; *vaiṣṇava-aparādha*, offenses against the Vaiṣṇavas; and *guru-aparādha*, offenses against the spiritual master. Let us not run from the opportunity to use the material energy in Kṛṣṇa's service, to become even a big administrator like Mahārāja Ambarīṣa, who oversaw the whole planet. After all, the *bahiraṅgā-śakti*, the external energy, and the *antaraṅga-śakti*, the internal energy, are arranged by the same Kṛṣṇa. At the same time, let us remember that the Lord always waits for us to make ourselves more available as puppets. After all, the same Kṛṣṇa with the same love has been available since time immemorial.

We understand clearly that this is a society based on solid faith. It is society in which we apply faith to bring about practical spiritual experiences, commitments, and lifestyles. That is, we engage in preaching our faith and then let the miracles come through. If the miracle is not coming through, it means that we are too entangled in the material energy. Therefore, we fail to connect with high-level love. Cast your mind back to time when a deep level of surrender was present. Undoubtedly, many miraculous events occurred beyond your abilities or those of the leaders around you. We have to activate that mood again, even more intensely, and allow the divine energy to take us beyond our own minds and intelligence. That is Kṛṣṇa consciousness: allowing our consciousness to be engulfed in Kṛṣṇa's desires and Kṛṣṇa's aspirations. Then it falls upon Kṛṣṇa to do the necessary when we fulfill His desires.

Lightening the Burden of the Spiritual Master

In conclusion, we want to clear ourselves of gross sinful activities. We want to remove ourselves from subtle contamination, too. We want to feel always that we are not ready to receive God's love, but at the same time we cannot go another day without it. We cannot think of spending another year without being able to experience deeper levels of Kṛṣṇa consciousness. This kind of longing should keep us continuously in an emergency consciousness, ready to take out the *māyā* in order to allow Kṛṣṇa to come in. And with such a service attitude, we do our part in relieving Lord Caitanya from the anxiety of trying to help the conditioned souls. We stop wounding Śrīla Prabhupāda. We allow ourselves to be wonderful sons and daughters, grandsons and granddaughters.

Prepare to go back to the spiritual world today. Just as when we desire to travel within this planet, we prepare ourselves ahead of time. Before embarking on a trip, certain activities become distinct priorities, while others are no longer important. Now we are preparing to return to the spiritual world. Let us reassess our priorities. Are we ready to go? Have we made serious preparations? Have we already made ourselves available to fulfill Kṛṣṇa's desires? If we have truly made ourselves available, then we are already living in the spiritual world. We cannot procrastinate with the idea that we will pack later. We cannot go to the airport without our tickets and think we can fly. When we have thoroughly prepared beforehand, then the transition to our planned destination is very natural. These wonderful scriptures give us the formula of how to prepare ourselves. We are ready for happiness or distress. Even when the distress comes, we want to pray. Even when we are wounded, we are able to use that circumstance to glorify Śrīla Prabhupāda and Kṛṣṇa even more, not less.

If we saw somebody hitting or kicking Śrīla Prabhupāda, we would be furious. But in our own lives, many of us are actually attacking Śrīla Prabhupāda on a subtle level. How so? By receiving his gift and then forsaking that gift in so many ways. Ask yourself to what extent you are adding to the weight that Śrīla Prabhupāda has to haul up the steps, instead of relieving him of it. My sincere prayer is that I too will learn to stop wounding the spiritual master, that I will become skilled at lightening his burden as I watch all of you remove each and every one of his heavy bags.

Question: Does Kṛṣṇa feel pain when He sees us bewildered by the material energy?

Answer: That is a very nice meditation. Kṛṣṇa cannot be wounded in the material sense, but just as a father who sees his son taking drugs naturally becomes worried, or a mother who hears her daughters fighting with each other becomes anxious, so too does the Lord feel concern when He sees us wallowing in the material energy. When you yourself have given your children an order and find it was not carried out, how do you feel? Knowing it was a healthy instruction for their well-being, you cannot help becoming disturbed due to your love for them. Some parents say, "I love my children; I let them do as they want." This is not love. True love means being happy to see our children behaving in ways that will be beneficial for the family and for themselves.

Parents naturally become upset when they know their children are doing harm to themselves. And this is also the position of Kṛṣṇa. Kṛṣṇa has such love for us that He allows us to undergo difficult situations in the hope that we will be inspired to rush back even faster to receive His love. Of course, the father is much more satisfied when we put ourselves in situations to receive all of his love. When we engage in deviations, we do not get all the love. Deviation means putting up barriers which prevent much of the love from coming through.

Question: How do we meet the demands of management in our organization without claiming proprietorship?

Answer: Śrīla Prabhupāda instructed us that good management means to keep everybody engaged. We have to agitate our minds as to how to do that in a loving way. A temple is not like a marketplace or hotel, where we try to fulfill everyone's needs and desires. We all volunteer to commit ourselves for the benefit of the whole. We all must make some sacrifice. At the same time, we must engage ourselves and take the engagement of others seriously. Otherwise, *māyā* will take advantage of the situation.

I understand that engaging others according to their propensity is not always easy, especially when managers are faced with man- and womanpower shortages and financial difficulties. Nevertheless, as managers we must bear in mind that when people are engaged according to both their ability and their interest, they make the greatest contribution to society. Usually when we are engaged in a service for which we do not have a propensity, we do it grudgingly or without sufficient zeal or attentiveness. We want to be available to do the needful. Yet, as managers, we want to try as best as possible to engage people in an area where they have talent, and moreover to train them up satisfactorily in that area.

Question: How do we get proper devotee association if we need to work and cannot reside in a temple?

Answer: Our scriptures reiterate that as one enters into an environment, one gradually becomes absorbed by that environment, unless one is a *paramahaṁsa*, a person on the topmost stage of spiritual advancement. Association is crucial: that is why we have the books and the audio recordings—and we have one another. That is why it's important to remember that our actions, our words, and our thoughts will enhance someone else's ability to run towards Kṛṣṇa faster. We all owe it to one another to associate in such a way that consistently reminds us to become more serious in Kṛṣṇa consciousness. If we find ourselves in an environment where only poor association is available, then our position is even better, in one sense. Now we have a chance to become that higher association for others. Kṛṣṇa will be there for us. This time, His mercy will come through even stronger.

Every day we go out and interact with so many people, and by so doing, immediately we exchange mentalities. We literally take *karma* from such associations. Therefore, we must constantly replenish our devotional reserves. We are in constant danger, working in secular environments, being bombarded by people who literally hate God or want to deny God. By such association, we become ingrained further in the matrices of power and control. By entering into the life space of those who do not desire Kṛṣṇa, we enter a negative force field, and literally attract contamination. Therefore, we must rejuvenate ourselves in the morning and at night by good *sādhana* and the best association we can find.

Question: Sometimes we find ourselves in a management position, but then realize we do not have a natural propensity for the service. What should we do in that situation?

Answer: Sometimes very good managers can be obnoxious people, while very poor managers may administer the strongest temples. We want to try to excel in both areas: organization and personal character. Let us become very powerful in encouraging devotees to surrender by our own example. Let us run our facilities well in order to make the grandest offerings possible to the *paramparā*. Even if we do not possess the material skills, if the devotion is strong enough, then Kṛṣṇa will come through. Kṛṣṇa tells us emphatically in *Bhagavad-gītā* 9.22:

ananyāś cintayanto māṁ
ye janāḥ paryupāsate
teṣāṁ nityābhiyuktānāṁ
yoga-kṣemaṁ vahāmy aham

> But those who always worship Me with exclusive devotion, meditating on My transcendental form—to them I carry what they lack, and I preserve what they have.

Ultimately, we have to come to a conclusion in our spiritual lives. Is this entire process a complete lie? Have all the *ācāryas* misled us, even though they appeared at different times and in different places, all preaching the same message? Perhaps each and every prophet of the world's bona fide religious systems was delusional, and there is no real final goal? Either we have to accept that this process is a total fantasy and reject it, or we must consider that it offers universal truth, and now we are called upon to align ourselves with it. But maybe we still question whether it's possible to attain love of God. Either the Lord does not love us and He is not all merciful, or Kṛṣṇa loves us dearly. If we accept that Kṛṣṇa always makes good on His promises to assist us, then we must look at ourselves and consider why we are not properly receiving His love.

Question: How do we align ourselves with Lord Kṛṣṇa's love?

Answer: On this planet, heredity and environment constrain us heavily, much more so than we sometimes understand. While we are products of our previous environments and lifetimes, positive shifts take place in our lives as we accumulate devotional credits. Spiritual involvement is the biggest business in creation. Not that we want to be materialists and engage in devotion merely to accumulate credits, but it is important to consider that when we do what is recommended by *sādhu*, *śāstra*, and *guru*, and as we avoid the *aparādhas*, then we are assured of ever-increasing divine intervention.

If, however, we deny the existence of divine intervention, then we will rely on our intelligence, which is what *māyā* would like. The more we rely on our physical intelligence instead of our spiritual intelligence, the more we fall under the influence of the material arena. As we function based on material considerations, we become products of the arena of limitation and frustration. Let us remind ourselves that we are in the movement of the miracle. The miracle is the norm. Kṛṣṇa is constantly showing us that He is Yogeśvara, the Supreme Mystic. Let us move out of the way to allow Kṛṣṇa to come through. Let us show Śrīla Prabhupāda that we are prepared to take advantage of whatever wounds we have experienced in order to be able to glorify *guru* and Kṛṣṇa that much more.

Chapter 6

Dedicate This Life to the Lord

Finding True Love

When we love someone, the desire to communicate, to exchange gifts, or to spend time together may be very intense. We usually experience feelings of separation if our beloved is not available, if we cannot see or hear from them. When we allow ourselves to fall back in love with the Lord, this experience of loving and being loved is intensified exponentially. As we make prayers to the Lord, as we respectfully and lovingly address those special helpers who have an intimate relationship with the Supreme Personality of Godhead, we enter into the culture of true devotion. By falling back in love with Kṛṣṇa, we gradually become candidates qualified to enter the realm of pure love.

When we are constitutionally situated, nothing is more important to us than receiving the love of God. If our real priority is to become situated in our constitutional position as loving servants of the Supreme Personality of Godhead, then spiritual life becomes so easy. When pleasing the Lord definitely becomes our priority, we inevitably begin to have ongoing contact with the spiritual realm. Keep in mind that Kṛṣṇa and His agents want to connect with us much more than we want to establish a bond with them. The Lord's helpers are always attentive to us, reaching down for us further than we are ready to reach up. If we genuinely increase our efforts, literally putting God first in everything that we do—not just theoretically, but cent percent—then the proof of our sincerity manifests in the direct experience of what previously we had only read about in the *śāstra*. The spiritual world becomes a real part of our own lives. We begin to relate in a meaningful way with the eternal arena.

I ask you to dedicate this one life to the Lord. I do not want you to undergo the process of *saṁsāra*, of repeated birth and death, any longer. Engaging wholeheartedly in the process of *bhakti* is not too difficult a sacrifice for attaining eternal existence. To be free of enemies, once and for all, to be permanently liberated from ongoing negative bombardments that we are forced to face every single day—whatever price we have to pay for that, it is worth it. Even if we have to live every single day in anxiety and frustration, being misunderstood, it is worthwhile because of what is ultimately attainable. If the goal is not wonderful, then of course, it is not desirable to pay a heavy price. If the goal is not permanent and we have to ultimately give it up only to enter again into the many complications from which we ran, then it is not a very captivating aspiration. But, if the end result is that all suffering is destroyed—death, disease, old age, and constantly living in an environment in which we have to struggle to survive—then it is worth it. Let's put all of these unpleasant experiences behind us by dedicating this one lifetime to God with no strings attached.

Material Time versus Transcendental Time

Sometimes we feel that the whole world is against us. Sometimes we may even believe that the Lord is also not responding, that He has forgotten or forsaken us. However, we know (at least theoretically), that the Supreme Lord has His own time scheme. The Lord knows what is best for the perfect unfolding of every single person. When we feel displeased because our lives are not unfolding according to our personal time scheme, we can reflect that Kṛṣṇa is momentarily hiding from us. By seemingly not receiving the Lord's mercy, at least in an obvious form, we will merely appreciate it even more when we finally uncover it.

In our day-to-day lives, we anticipate wonderful events or exchanges, which frequently take time to manifest. While reflecting on a future happening, a certain amount of maturation takes place inside. Then if the long-awaited event does occur, we receive it with a deepened sense of appreciation. Sometimes, we may experience such magnificent association with an inspiring mentor or a close friend that we constantly meditate upon attaining that association again. Often, we are able to continue from day-to-day merely by thinking about the previous times we were together. Reflecting on wonderful experiences carries us through. We can reflect likewise about our future association with the Lord and His devotees. It is very difficult being in environments where people are situated in materialism, individualism, and often voidism. Being on this planet is very difficult for those trying to develop devotion and selflessness, for those who want to stop running from the Lord and start running toward Him. In challenging situations, we can remind ourselves that our original, constitutional position is one of pure consciousness within a spiritual world where the love never stops. Just meditating upon our rightful claim—though we may not have access to it right now—can help us move through the temptations and the troubles of the present.

At the moment, it may seem that our suffering is endless, even if it is just one day or one week or one year when things are not going our way. However, let us consider that even millions of years comprise only a tiny fraction of eternal time. Once we are back in the spiritual environment, the millenniums during which we were away will seem like the flickering moments of a nightmare. Even though we have endured not only this life but many other lifetimes traversing the lower modes, once the soul is back in the spiritual kingdom in its natural state of *sac-cid-ānanda-vigrahaḥ* (eternality, full knowledge, and bliss), then the time that that soul was wandering from body to body and universe to universe will appear like a microsecond.

Therefore, when we find ourselves in situations in which we appear to be suffering, with complications far more than we can bear, we can almost laugh and realize that at some point in our evolution, we will have a chance to become pure and look back at the thorny past as an insignificant daydream. Remember when you were in school, and perhaps you would doze off for a few minutes? Maybe you were only asleep for a minute or two, but in your mind it was as if you were experiencing weeks or years? In one sense, it is as if we are in the spiritual world right now, but have nodded off for awhile. We immerse ourselves in the experience of nodding off here in the material world. It seems as if the complications, the miseries, and the challenges are never ending. But really, they are only moments in eternal time, just a temporary distraction, a momentary dullness in the realms of limitations. We constantly try to master limitations in the material universes in different forms, in different races, in different tribes, in different genders, lifetime after lifetime.

By turning away from relative material time, we can better understand transcendental time. Transcendental time can only be appreciated through knowledge of the soul. When we are suffering more than we can bear, when we think that things are just not going right, when we ask ourselves when they will stop, or how long we are going to have to experience this problem or that problem, remember that our suffering is only a fraction of a moment in eternal time. And as we alter our consciousness and become more transcendental, so will external events cease to be so depressing. Just as material techniques exist for engaging expediently with the physical world, so too is spiritual life a science—the highest science. Spiritual life is not to be undertaken with sentimental emotion, nor is it to be done by giving attention to the mind and the intelligence without understanding the properties of the soul. It is to be done constantly in the mood of *pravṛtti* and *nivṛtti*: appreciating the positive, while knowing how to avoid the negative.

Always be in a begging spirit. A begging spirit means making ourselves accessible to divine mercy, blessings, and intervention. We want to beg intensely, in order that our cries are focused, with great appreciation for what can come upon us when we do the necessary now. Do the needful to focus the mind. The mind can be our greatest friend, but usually it is our greatest enemy because it knows all of our secrets. The mind knows where we are weak, and it is familiar with our fears. The mind is expert in enslaving us to the senses. However, *bhakti-yoga* enables us to control the mind. When the mind stops interfering, we are able to feed the intelligence. Properly stimulating the intelligence opens up the soul, because all knowledge is contained within the soul. The whole process of self-realization is really nothing more than becoming natural again by moving the factors that cause stagnation out of the way.

Real Friends

Any knowledge that does not lead to wisdom, or any relationship which does not improve the quality of our devotional lives, is merely a distraction. Real friends help to remind one another of what is most essential. Real friends do not just stroke one another's backs or share poison together. Nowadays, in most cultures around the world, when people have not seen each other in a long time, what is the first thing they do? "Oh, come to my home, come visit me and let us take poison together!" Poison in the form of drugs or intoxication. And they consider that this is friendship. You have not seen your friends in a long time, so you want to know how they are doing while you slowly kill them. This type of social interaction is most unfortunate.

What is just as bad is when people come together and gossip or engage in faultfinding, activities which literally interfere with both individuals' evolution. True friends are those who connect with us spiritually, who encourage us to move faster towards the goal. True friends remind us by their own example of the benefits which come to those who remain faithful to the devotional process. If we are in a relationship that does not encourage us to run faster towards Kṛṣṇa, we should find a way of checking out of that relationship, because it is neither helpful to us nor to the person with whom we are associating.

The one who glorifies us is our enemy, while the one who criticizes us is our friend. The one who pats us on the back and says "it is okay" usually reinforces our false ego, while the one who finds fault helps us to realize that we have *anarthas*. If we are situated in the material realm, then we all have *anarthas* we need to work on. Those who remind us to do the intense work of *anartha-nivṛtti*, the clearing of unwanted dysfunctions from the heart, are our real friends. If someone praises us, we want to be careful to take their compliments in a mood of passing it on. We pass praise on to the Lord for allowing His mercy to come through, for allowing us to be used. Once we start owning glorification, then we must also own all of the burdens that accompany it.

Sometimes devotees inquire, "How can I know if I'm making spiritual progress?" It is a very common question. In one sense, the answer is simple. As we make spiritual progress, we notice that many activities which we used to find attractive now no longer interest us. People with whom we previously associated or places to which we were attached no longer excite or refresh us. Not only are we not attracted, but we begin to feel the opposite: that such environments have simply become a drain on our consciousness. Detachment from past activities is a positive sign that our consciousness has shifted. The same "you" goes into the identical environment, but it is not really the same "you" due to the inner processing you have allowed yourself to undergo. As we raise our consciousness, we no longer feel comfortable aligning ourselves with people, places, and activities based on our previous levels of awareness.

Spiritualizing Sleep

Even when we sleep, we want to use that time to learn more about the Lord. We want to serve Him and humanity ad infinitum. Consider that the average person spends a third of his or her life asleep. A lot of time is wasted! Higher level beings do not sleep in the ordinary sense. When they put the physical body down, they move into different environments and sometimes even into different universes in order to engage in higher services. As our spiritual life crystallizes, the soul, together with the astral body, receives great opportunities to do service which is not limited to time and space, the dimensions within which we are confined in the physical arena. The soul is not limited to the restrictions of the physical body in terms of endurance and other finite qualities.

When we can constantly put our bodies down to rest with a sense of zeal as we carry out services in the inner realms, then we can know that the physical body is gradually becoming spiritualized. The body no longer stagnates our striving for the higher aspects of existence. But if we find that in the subtle inner realms, our minds merely try to carry out the desires of the physical body, attempting once again to engage in the manipulation of the material energies, then we have much more work to do. Our goal is that the body and mind do not remain an interfering factor, but rather become assets in our service to the Lord and His devotees.

Before you take rest at night, ensure that your mind is in devotional consciousness. Read devotional literature for at least fifteen minutes before you go to bed. Engage in chanting and make sure that you put aside what has happened throughout the day, especially events which you found particularly distracting. We must prepare ourselves for entering this subtle but important part of our lives. Our waking consciousness directs what is going to happen to our souls and our subtle bodies while we sleep. Please run your life in such a way that enables you to both learn in the physical and to serve in the subtle. Make sure that you have relationships that constantly inspire you to come closer to the Lord.

Expect Miracles

Certain levels of God consciousness are so rare that we may enter into them by invitation only. Within the inner circle of spiritual existence, no imperfections exist. For a living entity to enter such confidential environments, he or she must be invited by those who are already part of these realms. Through high-level *bhakti*, certain blessings come upon us, bestowed by ambassadors of the Lord. Kṛṣṇa mercifully arranges the facilities of spiritual mentorship to empower us to reach levels of transcendence far beyond what we deserve merely through the quality of our devotion. *Śaktyāveśa-avatāras*, or devotees who are especially empowered by the Lord, literally descend to assist us in attaining direct association with the eternal servants of God.

This material world is far away from the kingdom of God, in the sense of what people do. Our patterns are so destructive that it is almost impossible to break out of this prison. If we found ourselves in prison with our hands bound and our legs tied, we could not do much to help ourselves. But if a savior somehow loosens the handcuffs, or releases a foot, then he or she actually gives us the ability to free ourselves from the rest of the shackles that bind us. Similarly, the agents of Kṛṣṇa assist us in breaking free from the shackles of material life. Their duty is to be on surveillance, to guide us, and to give us protection depending, of course, on the use of our free will. *Yogīs*, *ṛṣis*, and demigods such as Lord Brahma have various commissions and abilities to bestow undue mercy on living entities. At the same time, many more helpers who assist living entities in different environments based on different levels of consciousness are non-manifested. Our consciousness must be properly aligned for us to receive their blessings.

Generally, we hold ideas about space and time which are based only on this three-dimensional scheme, but actually the subtle patterns of all activities that have ever happened are still in existence. In fact, energetic blueprints of all that is still to happen are present right now in the universe. Therefore, it follows that the love of great helpers of the Lord is also ever-present. While Jesus, Buddha, Mohammed, and Vaiṣṇava saints like Śrīla Madhvācārya and Śrīla Rāmānujācārya may no longer appear on the planet, their love never leaves, even though the physical form they use may be manifest in another environment. As we cultivate more devotion, we will be able to connect with the presence of these pure entities. Devotion brings more devotion.

When we read *Bhagavad-gītā*, *Śrīmad-Bhāgavatam*, and *Rāmāyaṇa*, we should clearly understand that these scriptures are just as alive as we are. Never read the scriptures as if they are simply a collection of stories. We should not approach any type of holy book merely to derive data from it, but rather in a mood of appreciating it as a living, literary incarnation of God. To the extent that we engage with the scriptures in an appreciative, personal mood, to that extent will they take on a live quality for us. Some highly advanced souls read a few words from the scriptures and immediately go into a state of trance because their reading is not merely the viewing of words on a page, but in fact a powerful connection to transcendence. One of these great personalities, Śrīla Rūpa Gosvāmī, wrote many books about intensely deep aspects of God consciousness. His intention was to provide a window to the spiritual world. By approaching our literature with great devotion and care, we can eventually gain admittance to the very pastimes about which we now read.

Sometimes, when Śrīla Prabhupāda was manifest on the planet, devotees would become a little disturbed when he consistently gave one lecture after another, repeating, "You're not the body. You're not the body." Some of them would wonder, "When is Śrīla Prabhupāda going to speak about esoteric *līlās*, or pastimes?" Certain knowledge is confidential, to be experienced rather than spoken about. Reflecting on categories of the esoteric realm with the material mind and intelligence may lead us to distort truths regarding properties of the soul. We have to work on our characters and on our stagnations in order to qualify for the sublime experience that is ultimately available to every living entity.

Most highly elevated souls do not engage in parading their mystic powers, because they realize that it attracts people to mysticism rather than to pure devotion. Elevated souls are reluctant to do anything which will encourage people to think that self-realization is merely a matter of one technique or another, or of going to this group or that group. In essence, spirituality is a matter of allowing ourselves to infiltrate deeper into what Śrīla Prabhupāda has already given us. Sadly, we constantly avoid accessing what we profess to want, mainly because we are not so sure that the price to be paid is really worth the purchase. Therefore, we start and then stop, we dabble and then we move in a horizontal way instead of going deeper and deeper, trying to penetrate various levels of consciousness.

In *Bhagavad-gītā* 6.6, Lord Kṛṣṇa explains:

bandhur ātmātmanas tasya
yenātmaivātmanā jitaḥ
anātmanas tu śatrutve
vartetātmaiva śatru-vat

> For him who has conquered the mind, the mind is the best of friends; but for one who has failed to do so, his mind will remain the greatest enemy.

Lord Kṛṣṇa reminds us that our mind and our senses constantly incarcerate us. The mind is the cause of our suffering. Therefore, it must be transcended. We need to see what we have to shed in order to acquire what is necessary. This is the spirit of Śrīla Mādhavendra Purī, that a devotee is to be concerned about doing what is proper, but at the same time, he or she should not become puffed up by meditating on his or her so-called *pukka* execution of *śāstra*. We should feel that we can be forgiven of all our great sins only if great personalities petition the Lord. In the most esoteric sense, we have never left the spiritual paradigm; we have never stepped beyond the divine arena. Unfortunately, our present state of evolution causes us to identify with the temporary. We want to shed these shackles by first realizing what is accessible, and second, that it is our rightful claim. Pure happiness is accessible for us. When we allow ourselves to think that this state is outside of our jurisdiction, or that it is an imposition, then we bring incoherence into the devotional process. The knowledge that this state of purity has our name on it should enthuse us to acquire it.

In summary, when we really make God our top priority, miracles unfold. Realizing that we have to do our part, we trust that the mercy of the Lord's servants is always accessible. This mood of simultaneous endeavor and surrender allows us to move quickly in our devotional service, literally to shed great amounts of *karma*. The general tendency these days is to move very gradually towards Kṛṣṇa. However, if we move too gradually, we will not be able to run away from the *māyā* that is not gradual, that is running after us. By making the scriptures our life experience, by appreciating the great saints in various traditions (what to speak of those in the Vaiṣṇava line), and by realizing that they are there for us, we will attain their shelter and their love without delay. If we want our spiritual selves to unfold miraculously, then we must stop putting ourselves in situations which prolong the suffering, which extend the daydream, lifetime after lifetime.

Question: In the Christian religion, we understand that as a result of the transcendental work Lord Jesus did on the earth plane, those who follow him become as he was and become heirs to the spiritual kingdom on earth. One should carry oneself regally, as befits an heir to all that the Father has in store and all the rewards. If this is a valid spiritual concept, then how does it contrast with what you were saying earlier about carrying oneself like a beggar, in the mode of complete surrender to the Supreme Lord?

Answer: Just as different levels of love exist, so too do different degrees of God consciousness. When your love is not deep, you look at the object of your love in terms of what he or she can give you. It is like business: you do such-and-such and you expect such-and-such. Certain levels of attentiveness toward the Godhead involve a business-like mentality. We may pray, we may meditate, we may chant—and then ask, "Okay, now what are you going to do for me, Lord? It is your turn."

A higher level of God consciousness, however, considers the position of the object of love, rather than one's own situation and what one can get. Being intoxicated by what God can do for one, rather than trying to move into a situation of being all for the Lord, means we are still entrapped within the material paradigm. At the same time, if we are looking for wealth, distinction, or even mystic power, it is better to direct those desires to God than to be atheistic. Even if one tries to connect with the Supreme Personality of Godhead with contamination, gradually it will be purified as long as we persevere. It is as if God consciousness is a blazing fire: if you come close to it, you will get warm. If the fire is strong enough, it will absorb whatever enters into it.

In *Śrīmad-Bhāgavatam* 2.3.10, Śrīla Śukadeva Gosvāmī explains to Parīkṣit Mahārāja that even if you are full of material desires, it is best to turn to Lord Kṛṣṇa:

akāmaḥ sarva-kāmo vā
mokṣa-kāma udāra-dhīḥ
tīvreṇa bhakti-yogena
yajeta puruṣaṁ param

> A person who has broader intelligence, whether he be full of all material desire, without any material desire, or desiring liberation, must by all means worship the supreme whole, the Personality of Godhead.

If you have no material desires and you are on the liberated platform, it is still worthwhile turning to Kṛṣṇa. In any scenario, the position of the individual can be elevated. There is never a time when we reach a certain level in spiritual life and cannot go any higher. There is no such conception. Therefore, by increasing our desire to love, to serve, the Lord in the heart will perfectly arrange the environment for us to do so.

In the *Gospels of Matthew* and *Luke* in the *New Testament*, the beatitudes emphasize that the pure in heart shall see God and the meek shall inherit the earth.* In *Luke* 9.58, Lord Jesus says, "Foxes have holes, and birds have nests, but the Son of Man has nowhere to lie down and rest," emphasizing that when we take to spiritual life, sometimes we may be denied certain facilities. If material facilities constitute distractions, we should try to minimize them. Although people may mistreat us because of our faith, we, like Christ, must not back down from our sense of commitment.

Yes, humility combined with perseverance is an apparent duality. Nevertheless, this understanding of our relationship with God is ever-present in many spiritual traditions. It is not that spiritual people are docile. People who are just

* *Matthew* 5.1-12; *Luke* 6.20-23

religious may be docile, but spiritual involvement means intense investigation, powerful scrutiny, and concentrated evaluation of yourself and your environment. Spiritual involvement means no-nonsense consciousness. It does not mean that you distrust or abuse others because you think only about yourself, but it means seeing how you and others are related as parts and parcels of the Lord. This material world consists of the separated energies of Kṛṣṇa, including His lower energies. Realizing how this world constitutes a prison will naturally humble us. We remain prisoners, no matter what type of cell we may acquire.

Question: What does it mean to be born into a good spiritual family?

Answer: A good spiritual family will provide an environment that exposes the child to spiritual stimulation, even before he or she comes out of the womb. And after leaving the womb, the family encourages the child to continue onwards with his or her spiritual evolution. Prior to the soul entering the womb, the mating itself is done in such a way as to attract souls of higher consciousness.

A soul who wants to make serious progress in spiritual life will not be eager to take birth in a family which is atheistic, or one which will interfere with his or her particular growth. The *karma* of a particular soul dictates a need for a particular type of environment which will allow it to experience what is necessary. Nowadays, most people are involved in illicit relationships. They have sex without wanting to be accountable, using contraception and sometimes even aborting the fetus. From a metaphysical perspective, this kind of sinful action results in a tremendous backup of souls who want to come into this world, and an even greater backup of souls who are spiritually inclined.

Sometimes when spiritual people fall down due to sex agitation, it is due in part to the desire of a soul who wants to take birth from their union. The unborn soul knows that a particular man and woman would create a nice body for his or her spiritual development. Therefore, the persons whom that soul views as potential parents will feel agitated. That soul does not care whether those people are married, or even if one is married to someone else. It merely seems as if those two people together could make a certain type of body that the particular entity would like to have for its progression. All over the world, in all major organizations and religious institutions, people are falling prey to sex agitation. Much of this problem is due to the new era of certain advanced types of souls trying to take birth on the planet. Most individuals do not know how to deal with this situation. It creates anxiety and especially embarrassment if the two parties act on their feelings of agitation.

Question: What are the ramifications, if any, of undergoing artificial insemination?

Answer: There are many consequences to undergoing this procedure. A major consequence is that a woman will probably not know the connection between the particular sperm used to create a child in her womb and the person who donated it. To carry an entity without knowing the consciousness of its father is very risky. Sex life is for procreation. Ideally, a couple should come together as a service for the Lord, to bring into the world a soul whom they are ready to caretake as servants of the Lord. The couple should also be willing to grow through this experience.

Adoption places one in a similar scenario to that of artificial insemination. You could adopt a child without knowing who his or her parents are. Realize that tremendous connections exist between that particular soul and the man and woman who participated in producing its body. If one is ready to deal with the implications of this knowledge, then she can go ahead and adopt a child, or undergo artificial insemination.

Question: In the *Śrīmad-Bhāgavatam*, we read of many cases of children born out of wedlock, some of them elevated souls. For instance, Parāśara Muni had union with Satyavatī prior to her marriage to Mahārāja Śantanu, which resulted in the birth of Śrīla Vyāsadeva. There is also the case of Viśvāmitra Muni, who begot Śakuntalā in the womb of Menakā. In fact, King Indra specifically sent Menakā, a beautiful *Apsarā*, or denizen of the heavenly planets, to seduce Viśvāmitra Muni, who fell down from his position as a mystic *yogī*. Are illegitimate births actually arranged by the demigods, or do they result from the desires of the unborn souls who want a particular type of birth?

Answer: Both the demigods and the unborn souls have parts to play in engineering these scenarios. *Śāstra* tells us that sometimes the demigods perceive that a certain soul is in a position to occupy one of their posts, and therefore they may cause interference with that soul's progress by tempting him or her to engage in illicit activities. Sometimes, however, the unborn souls themselves are in need of a particular kind of body. An entity in need of certain guidance will want to take birth in the womb of a particular being that he or she chooses as a mother or father. That living entity will put pressure on the consciousness of the potential man and woman when they are in association. If one is not firm in one's vows, then one will find the sexual energy overwhelming. There is every chance of a falldown.

In no way does the pressure exerted by the demigods or the unborn child constitute a rationalization for a falldown. I am simply identifying factors which sometimes cause constant stimulation when spiritual people are in association. Since we function within environments where we are programmed to associate love with sex, if we are not careful, everyone will be lusting after everyone else, and calling him or her their "soul mate". Every year we will have a different "soul mate"! One has to know that yes, in a spiritual environment, we will experience a natural pulling. We should not feel ashamed, but rather understand that we need to handle this energy in a way which does not cause a disturbance.

Question: Frequently, we are bombarded by thoughts of sex from the conscious mind, the unconscious mind, and from subliminal suggestions that enter our environment daily. Now you're telling me that unborn souls and the demigods are also exerting pressure on us! You have said previously that for us to live as hermits, who pray and worship in a solitary way, is not positive. What do you suggest we, as struggling souls, should do to counteract all these powerful influences?

Answer: I want to emphasize that going off to the Himalayas or to the bush is neither bad nor good. It is a matter of what one does when one retreats from society. If you go off to the mountains or to the cave and your mind is constantly thinking about ice cream and disco, then you might as well be at the disco! But if, in fact, you have the ability to do service in solitude, then it is good to be alone. The Vaiṣṇava tradition glorifies both the paths of the *bhajanānandī*, the spiritualist who practices in seclusion, and the *goṣṭhyānandī*, the spiritualist who is active in the secular world and assisting others. Particularly in this day and age, however, a great need exists for role models. People want to see practically how to conduct their lives in a God-centered way. Therefore, it is very important for genuine spiritualists to make themselves available as they proceed in their spiritual lives.

Interaction with others is also important for the spiritualist herself. Often the person who is living a life of seclusion may become disillusioned by thinking that he or she is stronger than he or she really is. We only really master a situation once we situate ourselves in an environment where we can be put to test. Salvationism, or absorption in mystical intoxication, is not necessarily a sign of advancement. When we are able to maintain a spiritual consciousness in a degraded or chaotic environment, then we show signs of real maturity.

Question: Do higher beings always have our best interests at heart? Is there a way we can receive messages from them directly?

Answer: Of the numerous demigods in our universe, some are deeply God conscious, and always try to act for the benefit of everyone. However, at times a demigod can become mischievous or deviant, much like a "blooped" devotee who was involved in a system which is legitimate, but has chosen to deviate from it. Besides the demigods, there are *asuras* or demons. Demons often wield the same power as the demigods, who are very powerful and mystically endowed, but they are literally bent on bringing about chaos and destroying God consciousness.

In the Christian tradition, we read about the sons of God mating with the daughters of man. Super-humans, lower than demigods, previously interacted on this particular level. The whole earth planet was originally seeded by higher beings. The entities that occupy this planet nowadays are not the original beings of this particular planet. One spiritual tradition after another tells us that previously human beings had bodies like giants and abilities that today would be considered supernatural. Nowadays, we are still subject to higher monitors who oversee our activities. These monitors are not necessarily spiritual beings, but of a higher capacity than ourselves.

What people now term Greek mythology, Roman mythology, and Indic mythology speak of times when there were ongoing interactions between entities on this planet and entities in the heavenly kingdoms. Currently, scholars term these histories "mythology," as they are blind to the fact that these narratives convey universal truths far beyond what they can comprehend with their present mindsets. During the time of Lord Buddha, interaction between superhumans and demigods with humans on earth decreased drastically, but before Lord Buddha's descent, priests would frequently perform *yajñas*, or sacrificial ceremonies, in order to invite higher entities to come to earth and interact with them. Previously, pious people had the ability to be in tune with universal governance and to be able to reciprocate appropriately with higher beings. But now the planet has become so thick with mundane collective consciousness that these entities are not eager to come. Many entities who were commissioned to work on this plane are no longer involved. Higher beings want to come to an environment in which they can relate.

But, even now, demigods will arrive if we have the appropriate consciousness to attract them. Once Śrīla Prabhupāda was preaching in New York. The devotees surrounded him, dancing and singing in *kīrtana*. Śrīla Prabhupāda seemed to be looking over to a particular corner of the room. He nodded and smiled, as if he were acknowledging someone whom the others could not see. Later, when Śrīla Prabhupāda went up to his room to retire, some devotees asked him what he was looking at and why was he smiling. Śrīla Prabhupāda mentioned that Nārada

Muni, a very powerful higher being, had appeared during the *kīrtana*. Due to Śrīla Prabhupāda's purity, Nārada Muni, a transcendental spaceman who travels to different universes purely for Kṛṣṇa's service, had appeared during the *kīrtana* to celebrate the pioneering of Kṛṣṇa consciousness in the West. Elevated beings such as Nārada can come based on the quality of our devotion. We can all pray to improve our personal qualities to such an extent that gradually we can qualify to contact the transcendental realm.

One does not have to wait until he or she leaves this physical body to know that God consciousness is alive and real, to believe that there are demigods, or to believe that even the Supreme Lord can be approached. Those experiences are accessible to us now. As we develop the consciousness of the higher realms, we begin to unfold and lose some of our soul's dormancy. We are currently situated in the spiritual kingdom, with wonderful spiritual connections, but we are sleeping. The spiritual process is like waking up—it allows us to experience what is already present. Remember that for one to have contact with higher realms is natural and to not have contact is unnatural.

Question: Is there any spiritual merit to the philosophies of various *yogas* which advocate using the sexual urge to raise the *kuṇḍalinī* in a morally acceptable situation between two partners without the anticipation of childbirth?

Answer: Bona fide systems of *tantra* are based on control of sex energy, not on promiscuous use of sex energy. Controlling sex energy according to certain yogic systems can result in the development of mystic power. Vaiṣṇavas, however, control sex energy for the purpose of developing love and devotion for the Lord. Unfortunately, many of the black arts utilize principles which lie on the left hand side of *tantra*. When properly controlled, sex energy is a catalyst for the ecstasy of *bhāva*, a very pure level of love of God. When one tries to harness sex energy for the purpose of developing supernatural powers and not for procreation, then one's actions border on the demonic. This type of engagement is dangerous.

In one sense, spiritual life is natural. We do not have to know many intricate spiritual laws and principles in order to evaluate what is natural. It is natural for a man and woman who are fertile and in a committed relationship to come together and procreate. When people pursue abortion and contraceptives, they interfere with the natural order of the universe and therefore have to suffer the consequences.

Question: During the sexual revolution, most people were looking for procreation for recreation, not realizing that they were really searching for spiritual bliss.

Answer: Yes, this attitude towards sex is a serious problem, in part due to Hollywood portrayals of relationships which constantly confuse love with lust. We have forgotten how to really care for and communicate with one another, other than through physical connections. This lacking in our relationships results in the experience of an intense ongoing inner emptiness. Because of their emptiness, people search for stimulation, and in the material world, stimulation usually means indulging in either drugs or sex. As people feel less and less fulfilled, nourished, or happy, their emptiness causes them to tune in to those areas. Promiscuity and incest are therefore on the rise, as individuals feel that they must be physically involved with those they care for. Drug use increases concurrently. It is an unfortunate situation.

At the same time, it is natural for us to experience ecstasy. It is a natural part of the soul to experience far beyond what is available in this particular body, in this particular world. Every individual is inwardly looking for ecstasy, but if we look for it in artificial means, then we place ourselves in great danger. The term "artificial insemination" immediately alerts us to a certain hazard. Demons do not only exist theoretically. No, demons are entities who demonstrate ongoing opposition towards the Godhead. If we think in terms of a demonic master plan, what better means is there to destroy or stagnate a large group of people than by enticing them to engage in an activity in a perverted way? It is natural to undergo altered states of consciousness, to experience a great sense of pleasure. People need and desire ecstasy. If you want to control them, there is no better way than to create a drug that gives them what they want artificially—simultaneously crippling them and making them dependent on you. Thus you can take them away from God.

Taking drugs affects the subtle body in so many ways. It makes holes in the subtle body, allowing negative influences to intrude. Drugs make us candidates for more and more degradation. They keep us from aligning ourselves spiritually. People who take shelter of drugs come from all political and economic situations, from all race groups. Drugs know no borders. Many major countries derive a significant amount of their foreign exchange from illegal drugs.

A massive war is being waged on the planet between pious and impious entities. Both groups are literally trying to win over converts. Impious entities want to prevent people from making a positive impact on this planet, and also from making a transition to higher arenas in their next lives. Therefore, the pious entities have to work to create situations and role models that will allow those who want to make a real difference in this lifetime to be able to see how to do so and to feel motivated to persevere in their efforts.

Question: Should a married man and his wife only involve themselves sexually when they are ready to have a child? Can this kind of conduct be also considered a form of celibacy?

Answer: Definitely. The most natural idea of sex life is one in which a couple is accountable and responsible. They come together as a team, as partners, to take responsibility for their progeny. It is up to the individual couple how strictly they follow the model of celibacy within a marriage, knowing that the more we please the Lord with our bodies, minds, and intelligence, the faster we get released from incarceration. The more we play the body game and keep the body from functioning the way it is supposed to, the more likelihood we have of taking another type of body to work out various karmic patterns. So yes, when people in fact do engage in sexual intercourse with the idea of procreation, with a legitimate mate, then that activity is also considered celibacy. In one sense, restrained sex life under these conditions constitutes an even greater celibacy than complete abstention.

Question: Some people use contraceptives and even abortion in order to be responsible about bringing children onto the planet. Think of all the problems we have with children who are not wanted or loved. Some people in loving relationships feel that sex is a spiritual experience, whether or not they choose to have children. Would you agree that preventing a child from coming when one does not feel capable of parenting properly is a sign of responsibility?

Answer: We must not confuse sociological considerations with spiritual ones. Sociologically or economically, we may not have the means to take care of a child, and that is a reality, but these facts do not change the spiritual dynamics of the situation. Spirituality means that when you give yourself to someone and they give themselves to you, both partners must be ready for the natural consequences that arise from that giving. Sociologically, we may not feel ready to handle a certain amendment to our lives, but if we want to be spiritually conscious, we must give priority to the spiritual reality and consider our actions from that perspective.

A real serious problem today is that people do not understand spiritual science, especially when it comes to procreation. As a result, the planet is over-populated with lower entities. Having sex without wanting to be accountable with someone who you do not consider to be your partner, many times under intoxications, in the dark, will not lead to a fortunate outcome. If we procreate in the lower modes, how can we expect that the union will bring forth something divine? Is a divine personality going to be attracted to coming to a place where they are not even wanted, to parents who do not consider the consequences of their actions, to self-centered people who just want their own satisfaction and use the other person as a pleasure unit? Do you think someone who is selfless, who is full of compassion and devotion, will be happy with the kind of body and home environment these entities are able to produce?

Let us become more thoughtful about what we do and how we involve ourselves in the laws of nature. Let us realize more profoundly that what is really missing in the world is love. Why do we get so distracted by so many material things, even by sex life itself? As soon as there is not sufficient sex life, people divorce or they lose interest because they equate love with lust. Do not be a slave to your tongue, do not be a slave to your mind, do not be a slave to your intelligence, and do not be a slave to your genitals if you want to be a free man and woman in a world that is a prison, in a body which is a prison. If we talk about liberation, we have to be ready to function as liberated entities. If we talk about going to higher realms, or to the kingdom of God, then we should live in a consciousness now that shows we qualify to live there. The more you live anti-materially now, the more you are ready to live eternally in your actual spiritual home.

Do not see spiritual life as an imposition. Do not see it as merely theoretical. Instead, try to see spiritual life as a real living situation, every day. Everything in the universe is personal. I gave the example earlier about how sexual agitation is sometimes due to living entities who want to enter into a particular environment. Inside your body, many living entities are evolving based upon how you function. Your body is a universe, even an atom itself is a universe. The universe itself is a living entity. Life exists within life. Many different types of amazing life forms attest to how dynamic existence is. Let us attempt to see behind the facades and perceive who we really are in terms of the soul. Living from the perspective of the soul means becoming less and less influenced by bodily demands. When we are captured by bodily demands, then that is a sign we are qualified to get more physical bodies, lifetime after lifetime. There is a particular reason we are born in a specific race, religion, and gender, based on issues we have to work out. But if we take our prison suit and our prison situation as the all in all, placing our entire concentration in dabbling within the prison, then we will just have to come back again as another type of prisoner. But as we think anti-materially, so will we align ourselves with greater pleasures. We do not want to be a part of what is happening in this material world.

With time, we will be overcome by great devastation and deterioration. The world is deteriorating at a very rapid pace. Those who do not cultivate spiritual technology will become casualties on this planet and will have to be recycled. Now we have the chance to get our lives together. This opportunity is a luxury. It is not going to be available for very long. Already, based on your consciousness, the *devas* are arranging your near future. Now you still have the ability to make serious progress in this particular lifetime. Do not put off your chance to work on certain bad habits for later, because you will not have time for that. Do not put off living higher principles because you feel the circumstances are not sufficient right now. If you are blessed with higher knowledge and you do not use it, it means you are self-centered and unappreciative. Refusing to apply God's blessings in your own life, and neglecting to assist others, you are considered a saboteur of higher consciousness.

Lastly, we should remind ourselves that the Lord never gives anyone more than he or she can handle. God is not unfair or insensitive. Whatever challenges we encounter occur for particular reasons. Similarly, it is upon us to see how we can give back our gifts to the Lord. If we have been given material facility, we are being watched to see how we are going to use it. If we have little facility, we are being watched to see how we cope with that situation. If you have a wonderful family, you are being watched to see if you are going to take proprietorship of them or if you are going to take care of them as devotees of God. If you are alone and you have no companion, then again, you are being evaluated to see how you react.

Instead of worrying and wondering about how to fill certain lackings in our lives, we should focus on what we have and try to use it in a way that God will be pleased. And when the Lord is pleased, then whatever is best for us will come gushing out, rushing towards us. Is it not better to try to adopt this consciousness, than worrying about our particular problems? Time is ticking away on the planet, and we risk losing our chance to make the deeper connections while it is still easy for us.

Chapter 7

Losing Oneself to Gain Oneself

Addressing Inner and Institutional Conflict

Do you find that after dedicating many years to spiritual life, you suddenly face tremendous inner conflict? Are you questioning your theology and your commitment? Is your community undergoing severe in-house fighting, despite the fact that it is meant to be based on spiritual principles? Take comfort in knowing that you are not alone. Throughout the planet, many of those who have invested veritable fortunes in their spiritual bank accounts find themselves encountering powerful challenges. Yes, we are under attack on a subtle level. At the same time, by exposing our weak areas, Kṛṣṇa affords us exciting opportunities to allow the science of spiritual life to work more deeply in our lives. However, to the degree that we refuse to cling closely to the shelter of the divine energy, to that degree will our minds be seized by these tremendous negative influences.

Problems are natural in all communities, in all orders of society. Just like personal difficulty, institutional tribulations come in cycles. We cannot fail to be affected by material dualities when we are not properly grounded in spiritual life. Just as a weight-lifter needs to train appropriately in order to cultivate the proper strength, so too do we need to develop our spiritual muscles if we are to stay the course. If weight-lifters do not properly prepare themselves before a competition, it is probable that they will hurt their backs or fall over when they attempt to pick up heavy barbells. Similarly, many devotees collapse spiritually when they find themselves unprepared to bear increased pressure on a subtle level. If we find ourselves in danger of falling in our spiritual lives, then we need to make better preparations. We have to strengthen ourselves. Most importantly, we must look through the eyes of *śāstra* at the areas in which we are lacking. If we take advantage of these wonderful times, we will become fit to wield increased spiritual weight successfully.

Mundane Morality Is Not Enough

In *Bhagavad-gītā* 7.4, Lord Kṛṣṇa explains:

bhūmir āpo 'nalo vāyuḥ
khaṁ mano buddhir eva ca
ahaṅkāra itīyaṁ me
bhinnā prakṛtir aṣṭadhā

> Earth, water, fire, air, ether, mind, intelligence and false ego—all together these eight constitute My separated material energies.

The whole material world is literally a manifestation of Kṛṣṇa's separated energies. As we break through the lower energies, we are given the opportunity to access higher ones. *Bhagavad-gītā* explains that each material element is ten times thicker than the previous one. The more subtle the energy, the more intensely one has to endeavor to overcome it. Of all the areas of separated energy, the thickest is the *ahaṅkāra*, the false ego. While it is true that in Kali-yuga most people experience trouble just overcoming gross sinful activities, serious spiritualists frequently discover that their subtle addictions to the material energy are even more difficult to combat. Anyone sincerely connected with a bona fide spiritual process must eventually strive to understand the authentic self in contrast to the acculturated self, the true self as opposed to the false self which constantly seeks sense gratification, whether gross and subtle.

It is in the very process of confronting subtle attachments that many spiritualists face embarrassment by falling down again and again. Frequently, we resist admitting our weaknesses even to ourselves, thus sabotaging our advancement. Almost always, our denial is due to the false ego. Until we understand how forceful is the challenge presented by the false self, we will not be able to advance without difficulty. In some of their writings, the great Vaiṣṇava *ācāryas* address the false ego as a separate person, an enemy within who knows our greatest weaknesses and constantly reinforces them. But if we connect properly with the process of transcending matter given to us by Śrīla Prabhupāda, we will undoubtedly penetrate through our material consciousness, our material body, and ultimately through all the material universes.

Why Many Spiritualists Fail

Many aspirants on the spiritual path never develop beyond the limitations of the false ego, and therefore they are able to access only a limited level of God consciousness. Remaining within the realm of imprisonment, their *ahaṅkāra* prevents them from experiencing the highest manifestation of reality.

For *ahaṅkāra* is rooted in misidentification. False ego means selfishness. Having a false ego means *ahaṁ mameti*, being focused on what we desire to experience. In essence, dissolving the false ego is unequivocally the most difficult problem for any spiritual seeker. But if we can transcend this subtle obstacle, we will realize our true nature as eternal and blissful spiritual beings.

Most spiritualists do not succeed in breaking the false ego. If they did, then we would not see so many falling down. In any tradition, there are more deviants than those who genuinely honor their theology—even amongst leadership. It is not that we fail to understand what is proper, but rather that we cannot apply ourselves sufficiently to break through subtle material barriers. After perceiving the epidemic proportions to which spiritualists are entrapped by the false ego, I was inspired to write *The Beggar III*. The main reason I write is for self-purification, as I want to advance constantly by becoming a better servant. The more we refuse to be captivated by the illusion, the better servants we can become. Any realizations I may have, I offer not only to Vaiṣṇavas, but to all other spiritual communities. We all must ultimately confront similar challenges.

Devotees of many faiths who cannot overcome the false ego become stagnant and eventually backslide. Backsliding means we are not experiencing the higher realms. The duty of a spiritual teacher is to give the highest knowledge. But if one is not experiencing transcendence, then how can he or she bestow it? A spiritual leader who is merely interested in followers is bogus. If he wants to access higher realms, but desires to keep others low, then he is simply an oppressor. Merely a part of the material nature, his role has little connection with transcendence.

Know without doubt that the greatest treasures await us if we stick sincerely to the path of *bhakti*. We do not have to experience death, disease, old age, or any type of confusion. Confusion arises due to the ambiguity of not experiencing. Lack of transcendental experience results in fear, manipulation, and exploitation—either consciously or unconsciously. However, if we allow ourselves to truly connect with more divinity, then we will naturally radiate spiritual energy, enthusing others wherever we may be. Constant contact with divinity means that we will no longer be compelled to shift periodically between our spiritual and material selves, because we are authentically connected with the spiritual energy. We discover that we are able to spiritualize whatever we do, and so become carriers of great *bhakti*. If we fail to surrender deeply to the process, however, then we minimize our enormous fortune. We find it almost impossible to deal with problems when they arise. One way to facilitate deeper surrender in the face of adversity is to learn about our legacy as Vaiṣṇavas. Our legacy alerts us to the possible problems we may confront on our spiritual journey, while at the same time it inspires us by invoking practical role models who magnificently overcame the illusion of the false ego.

Losing Oneself to Gain Oneself

In *Bhagavad-gītā* 2.71, Lord Kṛṣṇa advises Arjuna:

vihāya kāmān yaḥ sarvān
pumāṁś carati niḥspṛhaḥ
nirmamo nirahaṅkāraḥ
sa śāntim adhigacchati

> A person who has given up all desires for sense gratification, who lives free from desires, who has given up all sense of proprietorship and is devoid of false ego—he alone can attain real peace.

To claim our real identity, we have to lose our false identity. Often clinging tightly to false identifications, we block ourselves from retrieving our true selves. Ironically, in spiritual life, one must lose oneself to gain oneself. Or, as currently discussed in some management circles, one must undertake an activity with the end in mind. A professional musician, for instance, cannot allow himself to be distracted by what the audience thinks of his performance when he goes on stage. Merging his consciousness with the music, he performs optimally. Absorbed in a reality beyond himself, he later returns to his self-centered identity. Similarly, in the arena of sports, the best athletes envision themselves achieving their goals even before they set foot in the stadium. Athletic and artistic achievers absorb their minds in the attainment of their objective, not paying much attention to temporary setbacks which may occur while they are competing. A champion runner understands clearly that if she focuses on the pain in her legs or the cramp in her abdomen during the race, then she will lose.

Unfortunately, people allow themselves to be distracted by temporary upsets all the time. How often do we do this to ourselves? Notice how frequently we apply a winner's paradigm when we want to achieve a material goal, but how often we refuse to invoke this mindset in the service of the Lord. How much it would benefit us to let go of our temporary obsessions in order to gain the ultimate victory of a higher identity! We must give up our bodily identifications to discover who we really are. Not that we should be in denial, but we need to see our temporary designations as part of something much greater. Just as a musician does not dwell on every single note he plays, even though he acknowledges that they are all part of his composition, so too should we not identify too deeply with the particularities of our daily experiences, but absorb ourselves instead in the greater spiritual reality of which we will one day become a part. Depending on their relationship with me, people may address me variously as John, Johnny Boy, Toshombe Abdul, Ghanasyāma, Bhakti Tīrtha, or Swami Kṛṣṇapāda. But, at the end of the day, I know I must remove myself from all these temporary identities. I must lose these designations in order to acquire a higher sense of who I truly am.

How to Continue Year after Year

I am often asked variations of the following questions: "How do you continue year after year in your spiritual life? How do you avoid being disturbed by so many conflicts, institutional turmoil, and planetary instability?" To be honest, I am disturbed. Spiritual life is not easy for me. I find every day a challenge. Yet, I have managed to remain within the process due to the mercy of my spiritual master. I practice introspection rigorously. It is healthy to question ourselves periodically, to inquire internally, "To what degree have I become a distinct part of spiritual culture? To what degree does my particular tradition remain a theory upon which I ponder, but in which I do not fully believe? To what degree do I embrace our philosophy within my heart?" Everyone in the conditioned state is undergoing difficulties. At the same time, Kṛṣṇa assists each one and has no favorites. Although we may have different levels of *sukṛti*, or devotional credits, according to our past lives, each must pass tests designed by the Lord to perfectly fit his or her capacity.

A surefire way to remain fixed in devotional life is to perform constant inventory of our progress and commitment. I personally undertake monthly inventory, yearly inventory, and even inventory by decades. I also closely examine the behavior of those who are advancing steadily. I ask myself, "What are they doing that I am not? What is working for them?" As spiritualists, we should expect to personally have the experiences of transcendence promised by our individual traditions. Each one of us can absorb ourselves more and more in God consciousness. Unequivocally, some people on this planet will become God conscious in this lifetime. Let us aim to include ourselves in that quota. It is possible. The Supreme Lord is fair. He has not made our paths so difficult that no one can attain Him. Commit to becoming God conscious. Ask yourself, "What can I do today to speed up the process?"

Today I Died

For many years, I would frequently begin my diary entries with the following words: "Today is the last day of my life. Today I die." After making my submissions to my spiritual mentor, Śrīla Prabhupāda, I would anticipate what I would do in the remaining minutes before I was to leave this planet. I consciously made an effort to try to take each day in the spirit of it being my final time on earth. Any kind of austerity can become mechanical and therefore diminished in potency. Have you ever meditated on the moment when you have to leave your body? If this is the last opportunity you have to relate to certain people and do certain things, will you honestly be able to leave with a sense of completion? Remember that our state of consciousness at the time of death determines the quality of our next life.

Sometime later in my devotional career, I began trying to write in the spirit of Vāsudeva Datta or Lord Jesus. I would imagine suffering for others in order to release them from their pain. Recently, I was reflecting that I feel very happy in my spiritual life. Externally, I am experiencing more sickness, but internally, I feel extremely blissful. Each year, I grow more Kṛṣṇa conscious (hopefully, this is not an illusion). I feel more excited about what Śrīla Prabhupāda has given us. I feel more positive about the uniqueness of our connection with Śrī Rādhā and Śrī Kṛṣṇa. The more that I study other religions, philosophies, and cultures, the more thrilled I become about the immense value of our own heritage.

My intention here is to call attention to certain spiritual technologies that can assist enormously in resolving problems. I emphasize that whatever offenses I have made, I have to clear them up now. Whatever grudges I am holding, I must address them now. Whatever phobias I am taking shelter of, I must look at those now. Whatever offerings I must make, I must do those now.

I do not wish to present a morbid mentality, but rather a mentality which recognizes that we all have to leave. We are definitely going to give up this body. It doesn't matter how intelligent we are. It doesn't matter how much wealth we have. It doesn't matter how famous we are, or how much we have accomplished. None of that changes the fact that we all have to go sooner or later. We all know this. Yes, we have to plan—but to what degree do we really base our lives on the fact that our plans may mean nothing tomorrow?

Today, tens of thousands of people who had no idea that they were going to leave, died. They had so many plans for making money, traveling, connecting with people, expanding their material comforts—and now it all means nothing. Keep this simple fact in mind as you read the rest of what I want to share with you.

The more we address the false ego, the more we become transcendentalists rather than religionists. As religionists, we make demands of God. As transcendentalists, we want to meditate on how to remove material interferences. How much are we ready to move outside of the duality? The false ego will keep jumping up as we engage in our practice. This is a chance to look closely at ourselves and to ask:

"To what degree am I really grounded in bodily and mental consciousness rather than spiritual consciousness?" We hear about death and talk about it somewhat, but now let us bring that understanding home. If I have to leave tomorrow, what does that mean for my husband or wife, for my children? What does death mean for my plans, what will it really mean for me? We have to ask ourselves these difficult questions.

What Is My Status?

When people say nice things to us, usually we become very excited. But when people ignore us, criticize or challenge us, do we become sad, depressed, or angry? If so, we have a lot of ego to deal with. If we are really serving genuinely, then we feel happy whether or not we receive recognition. When we hear criticism of ourselves, it is possible for us to receive it with excitement. We can meditate with gratitude, thinking, "Here is a person who can help me to see how to improve."

Think about the last time somebody ignored you, criticized you, denied your existence, or challenged something you said or did. What was going on in your consciousness? Were you ready to embrace the feedback as Kṛṣṇa's mercy and to implement it immediately? Were you in the spirit of *dāsa-anudāsa*, of being the servant of the servant, by thanking that person for making such an offering? Or did you feel angry and insulted? Did you think about how to retaliate? Did you just start looking at that person's faults and think how much better you are? We must look closely at our consciousness, because we are all going to die soon—even if we live to be one hundred years old.

Let us each assess our own status. Our status means what we think and do every day, in every interaction. We have to examine ourselves and hopefully muster the conviction to be honest, to be truthful. When we notice that we are below the mark, we should work on it. Kṛṣṇa gives us numerous opportunities to see ourselves, particularly through the interactions of *sādhu-sanga.* Saintly people interact specifically to draw out the best and the worst in one another. Saintly people interact to remind one another of the goal—hopefully by example first. They interact to discover how they can become qualified to serve the Lord, to see how they can come forth to help, and how they can honor the help they receive.

Sometimes, even in devotional communities, people hold grudges. They decide, "I don't want to talk to that person. I don't want to serve with that person. I don't like that person." This mentality has nothing to do with serious spiritual acceleration. A Vaiṣṇava is not even his enemy's enemy. If somebody chooses to be your enemy, and you decide to honor that mentality by reciprocating as their enemy, then that is a sign of your great attachment to the duality. It is a sign of the dominance of the ego. The ego makes us suffer. When it rears its head, we must address it without delay. Otherwise, the false ego literally takes over.

Kṛṣṇa is kind. If we don't listen or respond to Him, then He gives us more abrupt situations to help us see more clearly what our actual status is. Many of us don't really take notice of the mirror Kṛṣṇa holds up to us until it becomes so obvious that we can't turn away from it. We get ourselves into embarrassing situations. It is as if we are walking nonchalantly in a dangerous area and don't notice the danger until we trip. Once we trip and fall, and even seriously injure ourselves, then we realize that the matrix of material energy is actually a dangerous place in which to walk. This is the hard way to learn. Learning the hard way is very precarious, because sometimes when we get wounded, that wound doesn't heal quite so easily. Or sometimes when we get wounded, we engage in counterproductive activities as a misguided attempt to bring about healing. In other words, we take shelter of greater danger rather than of actual protection. Subsequently, many of us decide to jump ship. In most cases, one will hold onto the credits one has accrued in the past—unless one becomes offensive to the point that one loses those credits.

We know it is possible to become completely God conscious from a conditioned state. If we are aware of this amazing possibility, why not think, "I am going to be one of those persons. I don't want to miss the opportunity for acceleration. I don't want to take a back seat. I don't want mediocrity. I don't want to accept failure. I want to be a high achiever, which means that I will stop trying to do things based only on my own mind and intelligence. I now let a higher intelligence take over. I am willing to get rid of this false self that is following me everyday, which will eventually choke me even as I keep denying it."

Why I Write

I write these books for specific purposes. Firstly, for self-purification and, secondly, I write out of deep concern for devotional communities. It is a very serious time for spiritualists on this planet. Most spiritualists are both disappointed and disappointing. Do I say this because I am egotistical, or because I am able to scrutinize what is happening and have a desire to make a difference? You decide. Look at yourself and make an evaluation of your own motivations. Are they coming from your real self? Are your real desires to be connected with *guru* and Kṛṣṇa? Or are you motivated rather by transitory considerations?

We need to look at ourselves and ask, "Are there times when we can make a difference in bringing forth a greater sense of principle-centeredness, truthfulness, and divinity?

Are there times when we distinctly have a chance to make a difference but we choose not to?" The Lord in the heart takes notice and has created the opportunity. He has given us that chance and now takes notice of how we use it. Often we want peace rather than service. Do we look for the avenue that is going to be the least imposing on ourselves despite our ability to extend ourselves, to make a difference? Surrender does not mean a lack of self-esteem. Surrender does not mean that one is to be docile. Surrender does not mean that one is to be motivated by blind faith.

By introspecting and offering these meditations as a gift to other Vaiṣṇavas, I lay myself open to the criticism that I am merely thinking about myself. My intention in writing about myself, however, is to become a better servant for others. When we think about our problems in the spirit of service, then Kṛṣṇa's magic takes place. If we are to worry about ourselves, we should be worrying about how we can be in a better position to serve.

But most of us worry that we don't have money, we worry about our health, we worry about our house, and we worry about our time. Actually, we should be worrying how we can better serve *guru* and *sādhu*. But if I worry about my own concerns and it stops there, then I will attract more to worry about. I will bring more of the ego and the illusion and the confusion into my life and those around me. Look at your worries and reflect from what level they stem. We want to enjoy on the highest level by going beyond temporary sense gratification and relative material culture. We want to access the culture of *bhakti*. However, in most cases, people don't really want pure *bhakti*. That is why, at certain levels, they become stagnant.

Journaling and diarizing are very important. These activities can help us to examine carefully the trends in our lives. Ask yourself: "Am I still dealing with the same kind of problems year after year? Am I still trying to deny the real issues?" As we look internally, we can analyze what has to be eliminated, what we are seeing but, perhaps, not really seeing. As Śrīla Sukadeva Goswami instructs Mahārāja Parīkṣit in *Śrīmad-Bhāgavatam* 2.1.4:

dehāpatya-kalatrādiṣv
ātma-sainyeṣv asatsv api
teṣāṁ pramatto nidhanaṁ
paśyann api na paśyati

> Persons devoid of ātma-tattva [knowledge of the difference between matter and spirit] do not inquire into the problems of life, being too attached to the fallible soldiers like the body, children and wife. Although sufficiently experienced, they still do not see their inevitable destruction.

Thus introspecting, we may realize that Kṛṣṇa has been present all along, and all along He has heard our prayers. But unfortunately, we could not sufficiently hear Him.

Fear of Killing the False Ego

Many of the difficulties we experience are in fact Kṛṣṇa's communication with us. Since we refuse to hear His desires or to accept what He has made available, sometimes we have to hear Kṛṣṇa's communication in more indirect ways. This can be very painful. Dealing with the false ego is a greater challenge and arouses greater fear than even dealing with the death of the physical body. While most of us fear death, having to really address the false ego is even more frightening because so much of our identity is based on false conceptions. We have become acculturated to the ego not only from this lifetime, but from many other lifetimes. It is all part of our subtle existence. Every time death occurs, the physical body is gone. Death of the physical body equals the demise of one lifetime. But the subtle body continues lifetime after lifetime, carrying the soul to another experience, another realm of duplicity, of inadequate enjoyment, of running away from the Lord.

This is why spiritual life is so easy, but at the same time so difficult, because our false ego cannot be addressed if we approach it myopically, with false conceptions and improper motives. We can't cheat Kṛṣṇa. We can't cheat God. Socially, mentally, and even intellectually, we may be able to fool others and ourselves. But when it comes to false ego, we cannot gloss over the reality. It is the false ego which constitutes the major obstacle to our returning back to the Lord. It is the central interference in our spiritual journey. It is the main obstruction to our spiritual acceleration.

Universally, the false ego represents stagnation for anyone who strives spiritually. We cannot approach God while still holding onto illusion. The false ego says, "I do not really want to be with God. I don't want to pay the actual price. I deserve more for less. I want people to accept that I am more than what I really am. I want the maximum amount even though I invest the minimum amount." This is a seriously flawed mentality, contaminated with attempts to ingratiate the Lord.

First class devotees are not in denial. They are not caught up in romanticism, but realize who the real self is and what the real needs of the self are. As we experience problems but think less of ourselves and more of others, then Kṛṣṇa will intervene and take away our own problems. This is the Kṛṣṇa magic. God is always trying to give to us, trying to nourish us, trying to protect us, trying to share love. When we are not humble, the Divine Couple still tries to come through, but ego closes the door. So being humble means to open up the door and let that love come through. When we truly realize what has been passed down to us, we eagerly embrace it. In awe of the gifts bestowed upon us, we try to live up to them by fully experiencing them and keeping them sacred.

Kṛṣṇa will help us all. If our motivations come from the wrong place, then we will fail the same test again and again. If we do not shift, we will lose faith and start turning back to previous pleasures for a false sense of security. If we do not address the false ego sufficiently, we will find ourselves constantly unhappy, because the false ego chokes Kṛṣṇa's love from coming through. When that love comes through, regardless of whatever hell may be swirling around us, we will feel happy because the transcendental is never subservient to the material. When we become too depressed, and lose faith and our desire to read and chant our rounds nicely, we need to introspect and ask ourselves what is going on.

If we do not introspect, the ego will settle in and continue to absorb our energies in the temporary world, causing us to have to come back into material universes, into material bodies. But as we realize that we are all eternal residents of the spiritual world who have eternal relationships in dynamic spiritual association, we can reflect more on how many wonderful devotees have risen above the false identity. As we begin to tune in to such personalities, we identify with them and move outside of our temporary selves.

The physical body is not our identity. If we don't take care of it, then we are guilty of negligence. However, if we invest most of our energy in maintaining the body, then we allow the false ego to dominate. Although everything is perfectly arranged by the Lord, we alone possess the ability to take advantage of or minimize His gifts. Every problem that keeps one in the material energy is directly due to false perceptions.

Every sin, every fall down, and every stagnation is due to false perceptions. Conversely, every acceleration is due to the enhancement of clarity of perception.

Withholding Love Means Cheating Ourselves

Recently, a young disciple wrote a letter to me, expressing that he was trying to live his life based on what he feels I would say, what I would do, and what he thinks may be pleasing to me. In one sense, his sentiments sound pretty fanatical. Is he denying himself his freedom of expression, or his idiosyncratic tendencies? Is he minimizing his own nature? In a material sense, this young man's desires are definitely signs of dysfunction. But in the spiritual sense, they can be the highest expression of love. When we really love someone, we constantly think, "What will be pleasing to my beloved? How would my beloved like to receive this offering? What can I do with them, what can I do for them?" Why? Because deep love is losing oneself to gain oneself.

We cannot love seriously if our motives are based on what we can get from other people and the environment. But as we lose ourselves in thinking so intensely about our beloved, less and less of what we want for ourselves becomes important. When direct reciprocation occurs, the experience of love is very powerful. Yes, people are afraid to love deeply because they are not so sure that the other person is going to reciprocate, or they are afraid they might get exploited (as in many cases they will). Therefore people are a little shy about the degree to which they lose themselves. If we do not lose ourselves, we cheat ourselves. The more we hold on to our temporary identities, the more we defraud ourselves out of our highest expressions, our highest pleasures, and our greatest opportunities to experience the deepest sense of union.

People all over the planet are currently cheating themselves because they are afraid to really open up, no matter what form the relationship takes. Whether relationships involve family, business, friendship, or romantic love, people are afraid. They are afraid that if they give all of themselves, they will not be met on the other side. Reluctance to open our hearts imposes a big problem, because ultimately we cannot connect with the Godhead without losing this temporary identity. We cannot connect with the highest source of love without becoming pure love ourselves. Deep love involves madness—a constant meditation on one's beloved, an ongoing constant desire to honor and to serve. The more one serves with all one's heart, the more one begins to feel wholeness. No longer are we putting our higher expressions on hold. Finally, we allow our higher expressions to be expressed in ever-increasing spiritual reciprocation.

The Dangers of Not Loving

Imagine what is happening on this planet, where most people find themselves unable to offer their highest expressions. Most of us tried in the past, but our love was dishonored. We put ourselves out there, but there was no one to catch us. And then we began to think, "You don't do this. It is not a reality. Giving your heart is just a concept based on Hollywood fantasies. It is something that people do as pretension or as drama. It doesn't really exist." Therefore, it is ultimately posturing that goes on now. Although many of us have undertaken a spiritual commitment, we have been conditioned by the mentality of our environment. We are conditioned not to give our hearts, and therefore it becomes hard to be all for the Lord. Actually, we don't know what it means to be all for anything. This refusal to give fully makes spiritual life very, very difficult.

It is no wonder that people are getting more physical sickness. As they shut down much of their higher nature, disease begins to eat away at their physical and psychological existence. So many diseases, so many physical and psychological problems are inextricably linked with our inability to absorb ourselves in the explosion of love and selflessness which is ultimately spiritual. The aspiring devotee whom I mentioned earlier is sincerely trying to connect with spiritual mentorship. His desire to surrender to a higher guidance is dangerous, but also powerful. The most powerful spiritual processes are extremely dangerous, but at the same time, extremely potent.

Have No Enemies

In *Bhagavad-gītā* 12.13-14, the Lord instructs Arjuna:

adveṣṭā sarva-bhūtānāṁ
maitraḥ karuṇa eva ca
nirmamo nirahaṅkāraḥ
sama-duḥkha-sukhaḥ kṣamī

santuṣṭaḥ satataṁ yogī
yatātmā dṛḍha-niścayaḥ
mayy arpita-mano-buddhir
yo mad-bhaktaḥ sa me priyaḥ

> One who is not envious but is a kind friend to all living entities, who does not think himself a proprietor and is free from false ego, who is equal in both happiness and distress, who is tolerant, always satisfied, self-controlled, and engaged in devotional service with determination, his mind and intelligence fixed on Me—such a devotee of Mine is very dear to Me.

Śrīla Prabhupāda comments in his purport that a devotee never becomes "his enemy's enemy"; rather, he thinks, "This person is acting as my enemy due to my own past misdeeds. So it is better to suffer than to protest." Even though someone may position themselves in an antagonistic way towards us, a person of divine consciousness does not honor that adversary as an enemy. A deep devotee does not identify with anything that is relative. He refuses to become distracted by someone who is behaving either as a friend or an enemy.

Śrīla Prabhupāda once took his regular morning walk when one of the gentlemen accompanying him became argumentative, rude, and later harsh. Some of the devotees were disturbed by this person's behavior, but Śrīla Prabhupāda merely remarked that he must have offended this man in a previous life. Even in cases where we may know that we are not in the wrong, or we may be totally bewildered as to why someone is positioning themselves as our enemy, we need to take the humble position. Those who have lost their sense of material identity do not honor the duality. Even when they sense the duality, they simply use it to access spirituality. In other words, they focus on love. They think, "It must be my issue. Maybe I did something to this person in a previous life. Or maybe I caused an offense of which I am not aware even in this life." They do not give in to hostility, to dividing the world into friend and enemy. They do not think, "I need to defend myself against this enemy, because, after all, he is attacking me." They have lost themselves to something higher. Therefore, their consciousness is stable because they are not engulfed by transient negativities.

Lord Jesus' Enormous Love for Judas

We can learn so much from the quality of dedication and love which great personalities like Lord Jesus exhibit. Pure devotees who immerse themselves in the bigger picture make their lives their message. They keep the end in mind, refusing to become distracted by other people's *māyā*, by the little obstacles that lie here and there. Pure devotees do not play the game of enemies and friends. Instead, they are in love with God and in love with their service to God. Therefore, they are able to connect with the God-quality that is genuinely a part of everyone, but which is put on hold in most cases.

As Jesus was carrying the cross, struggling to prepare for his own crucifixion, Judas made eye contact with him. As Judas looked in Jesus' eyes, he did not see someone who was angry about what had transpired. Judas did not see someone who was vindictive, who was ready to drop the cross on him. No. He did not see someone who was cursing him with vulgarities. Did Lord Jesus say, "How can you do this to me, especially you, my dear student, to whom I gave so much?" No. When Judas looked in Jesus' eyes, he saw only deep love and deep compassion. Judas cast his glance on one who understood the bigger picture. If anything, Judas saw compassion. He saw sorrow, and he saw gratitude.

It was not sorrow for Jesus himself that Judas saw in Jesus' eyes. By his expression, Jesus communicated gratitude towards the man who had betrayed him. Jesus seemed to be saying:

> *Thank you. Perhaps it could have taken much longer for people to gain a deeper understanding of what is spiritual. Perhaps my mission could have gone unnoticed. Perhaps those who never before felt the love of God will now understand. Our Lord is so loving that He sends His*

special agents even though they are misunderstood and abused, even though their lives are taken. Through my example, people will gradually understand the lengths to which God will go to try to reclaim those who are captured by false identity. Knowing that most of them will still not change, He sends his representative anyway. Although people abuse and misuse those He sends, the Lord constantly makes arrangements to assist us. And so you, Judas, you have glorified me to the highest, because you have put me in a situation where I can show that one must be ready to give all for the Lord. I can show to what degree one must not engage in identification with the temporary. Judas, I am an eternal being and those who envy me and wish me ill cannot stop me or stop my Father's mission. As a matter of fact, all they will do now is amplify the mission as people will come to worship and hear about me for the duration of this universe.

Jesus knew that the Pharisees and all of the cheating religious caretakers sent him to the cross because his life exposed their deviations. Such a great sacrifice by a great servant, who was sent by the same Kṛṣṇa, the same God, according to time, place, and circumstance, shows us the importance of not simply dwelling on our own sovereignty, our own protection, or our own idiosyncratic concerns. All of the eternally liberated beings are totally absorbed in their real identity, even as they come into this world. They do not allow themselves to get distracted by the fragmentations that constantly bombard us: racism, tribalism, political and economic discord. All this negativity may be around them, they may have to talk about it and move through it, but they do not identify with it. They honor it because they realize that a situation is understood by its negative as well as by its positive. They honor the discord as a force which enables them to amplify their dedication, their love, and their service to God.

Reassessing after Years in the Movement

If, after 25 or 30 years in the movement, we come to a point where we start questioning our whole existence, then we have reason to celebrate. Our doubts signify a chance to grow—if we are ready to be honest. If not, then the false self will jump right in, and we will search for all kinds of reasons to not address the real issue. We will point at others, at the situation, but we will not point at ourselves. Our future rests on our willingness to have faith in Kṛṣṇa's mercy. Our level of faith determines our ability to accept His love.

To lose our temporary identifications, we need to work and think with the end in mind. Great souls are sent by Kṛṣṇa. They offer their hearts, their association and take on a seemingly human quality. They bestow on us an amazing level of proximity, and then they leave. Their lives are messages from the Supreme Personality of Godhead. However, it is hard for the help to come through when misidentification takes root. When people are in need, but do not think they are in need, they will not take advantage of Kṛṣṇa's love. Even if they realize how grave the situation is, they usually will not do what is necessary to receive assistance. Many people minimize the importance of dealing first with the gross *anarthas*, and then eliminating the subtle.

Let us examine to what degree we have become immersed in transcendence. We should become just like the artist who has already envisioned his or her masterpiece, or the expert musician, or the chess player, or the sportsman. If an artist worries over each single stroke, he or she will experience difficulty. Successful artists already conceive of the outcome, and then move closer and closer towards that achievement. They immerse themselves in the experience of creation. Likewise, we want to immerse ourselves more and more in transcendence. Whatever we do, wherever we go, whatever we wear, we should know instantly that we are none of these identities. If we can genuinely embrace our true identities as servants of God, then immediately we move beyond the realms of duality that bring degradation, frustration, and pain. People are so wounded. However, if they allow themselves to identify with their true selves, then they will be able to develop the mindset of the young disciple who intensely desires to act and think in ways that would please the spiritual master.

Let us become able to properly honor *sādhus*. Let us look at the bigger picture. Everything has already happened. We are just waiting for the time element to reveal it. Let us lose our temporary identity and accept the greater holistic spiritual paradigm. We are all going to leave the body soon. However long we live, whatever part of the world we are in, whatever gender we are, we are going to leave soon. Whether in 100 years, in 50 years, or in 10 years—it is a short time. And if we have lived most of our lives already, we should look at ourselves and ask, "What will I do with these few years I have left?"

Question: Thank you for speaking about the necessity of dismantling the false identity. Along these lines, is it possible for the false ego to become institutionalized? Many of us have undergone the heart-rending experience of seeing leaders, whom we had previously idealized, fall down. It appears that instead of using the process of *bhakti-yoga* to dismantle the false identity, the institution itself supports the building of false identity.

Answer: Thank you for your astute observations. Yes, institutions very often maintain and propagate illusions. Institutions can do many, many unhealthy things. Ultimately, institutions are merely the aggregate of individuals who support a common ideal or purpose. When the majority of individuals allow their false egos to become dominant, then institutional structures will fall apart. Dissolution is a blessing in many ways. Just as pain alerts us to an imbalance in the body, so too does institutional disturbance send a message to us that we have to correct the deviation. Occasionally, however, a person suffers from a disease, but is not aware of its severity until he is near death. Sometimes, he dies from the disease. So, yes, these are genuine issues which must be addressed.

It is sometimes more difficult to address the institutional false ego because we hide behind dogma. We pretend to be a "company man or woman" when we are not genuinely committed to the company's principles. It is easy to get distracted by secondary issues and miss the real issues, just as occasionally doctors address only the symptoms of a disease, and not the disease itself. Frequently, when people encounter a problem in their institution, they search for a superficial solution. Institutions offer the facility for us to hide, to scapegoat, and to project. Just as institutions are powerful, so are they dangerous. Anyone who is unaware of the dangers inherent within institutions risks becoming a blind follower, someone who places too much emphasis on the rule of law without understanding the spirit of the law.

Question: I truly believe that most of us are genuinely trying to become spiritual warriors, but sometimes the mind rationalizes our deviations. How do we subdue the mind while we simultaneously try to become compassionate towards ourselves and towards others?

Answer: Many people find it very difficult to be compassionate to themselves as well as to others because they do not understand compassion. They have not experienced compassion even on a most basic level. When we do not understand what it means to be compassionate, we cannot be kind to ourselves, nor can we counsel others effectively.

Śrīla Prabhupāda said once that we should learn from the Catholic Church, in certain areas. Although the Catholic Church is undergoing many problems (even more than our organization, because their institution is larger than ours), it operates with a basic understanding that a person who intends to oversee other people's lives must undergo serious training. Their program of apprenticeship for pastoral care contains many elements which we could emulate. Just as psychiatrists are trained to diagnose the causes of a patient's illness as primarily biological, social, or psychological, so too should spiritual counselors in the Vaiṣṇava tradition become qualified to address obstacles in all areas. If we are pure enough spiritually, we can resolve any blocks. At the same time, in order to reach a level of purity, we first have to deal with psychological and social blocks.

For instance, let us assume that a devotee has a tremendous fear of surrender stemming from childhood patterns of abuse. Perhaps she had alcoholic parents and never felt protected by authority. At the same time, she is sincerely attempting to apply herself to a spiritual path. She tries to accept shelter, but simultaneously shies away from it because of the deep wounds in her psyche. It is difficult for this kind of person to embrace authority due to her past conditioning. We cannot just tell this sincere devotee, "Just chant Hare Kṛṣṇa and you will be fine." It is true that chanting Hare Kṛṣṇa eventually will cure all ills. At the same time, if a devotee has emotional issues which prevent her from chanting Hare Kṛṣṇa seriously, then those issues must be addressed. As devotees, we develop a certain lifestyle to support our following of philosophy. Both a study of philosophy and the development of a supportive lifestyle must be given proper attention. It is very difficult for a person to be kind to themselves when the basic patterns in their consciousness are destructive. She must seek the proper help, preferably from other devotees.

Śrīla Prabhupāda usually did not enter into the details of how to remedy psychological problems, or how to build an effective support system. He gave us the basic boundaries, which we are to use as guidelines to develop effective structures and procedures. We are to use our intelligence to find ways to fulfill his instructions within the constraints of time, place, and circumstance. Śrīla Prabhupāda did not have to elaborate in detail on how to distribute books: he merely wanted the books to go out, and he wanted us to find useful methods to fulfill his instruction. There was not time to delineate exactly how to raise our families, or how to build our communities, even though he wanted these duties performed expertly. When we act from a place of selflessness and humility, then so many connections will fall into place. Śrīla Prabhupāda himself said that in the mode of goodness, one knows what to do. But if the false ego is too strong, then we will be stuck in ignorance and passion. It will be harder to know what should be done, especially with ourselves.

Fortunately, if we continue chanting and following to some extent, the process will work on us despite our identification with the false ego. Sometimes, however, the process will work in a way that seems to cause us suffering. Most of us can recall times when we did not learn until the suffering became intense. Just like an alcoholic who does not take his addiction seriously until he hits rock bottom, so too do we sometimes need to undergo severe loss in order to properly address certain internal issues. If we refuse to deal with problems sufficiently due to our ingratitude, then frequently Kṛṣṇa will remove certain objects of affection from us until we learn to pay attention. Just as an alcoholic may remain in denial until she loses her job, her home, and her friends, so too may we need to lose many of the gifts Kṛṣṇa has given us until we are ready to admit, "Yes, I have a problem." The false ego causes us to make mistakes repeatedly, while we deny our errors and pretend (even to ourselves) that all is well. To be truly compassionate to ourselves, we must be willing to admit our faults and to seek to remedy them. Compassion for others means having the willingness to selflessly assist them in the same process.

Question: How do we understand the difference between the false ego and the real ego?

Answer: All knowledge is present in the soul, which is *sac-cid-ānanda-vigrahaḥ*. The soul knows everything, including our *svarūpa*, or our real identity. But to what extent are we truly ready to honor our real selves? It is the false self which invites the ambiguity that screens us from reality, plunging us into material life which is merely an arena for drama. So enraptured are we in the drama that we believe it to be reality, identifying the character we play as the self. The dramatic persona becomes a part of who we think we are. Just as pathological liars eventually begin to believe their own lies, so too can we rationalize a deviation to such an extent that we become totally convinced we are acting properly. Like people whose apartments are so dirty that they do not even see the dirt anymore, we accept certain characteristics which separate us from Kṛṣṇa. If we fail to cultivate sufficient humility and selflessness, we will not be able to see the dirt, to see our own failings. Instead, we will think, "Why doesn't God make it happen? Why doesn't He just eliminate my obstacles?" God is ready to remove anything that prevents us from reaching Him, but are we really prepared to let go of our stagnations? Will we merely bring them back if God removes them?

Experiencing trouble in spiritual life is similar to catching a cold. The germs are in the atmosphere, and if our spiritual immune system is compromised, our likelihood of contracting a disease is heightened. When we see someone who is weak, we should realize that we can also get sick. Maybe we have already contracted the disease, but we have not noticed. As we take inventory of ourselves, we can weed out unhealthy thoughts, habits, and behaviors before they take root. Sometimes, it is possible to avoid being infected if we are aware enough of our inner workings. Being truly selfless, humble, and brave evokes an inner certainty that we will be fine—no matter what happens around us. Inwardly, we discover great happiness and zeal. We will feel more conviction, not less. We will not start backsliding or find ways to justify deviating. We will not suddenly start questioning whether Kṛṣṇa is real after years of practice, or whether Śrīla Prabhupāda made mistakes. As we begin to identify the difference between the real self and the false self through daily introspection, processing doubts as they arise, our experiences in spiritual life will validate our belief in *guru*, *sādhu*, and *śāstra* and gradually diminish our investment in the illusion.

About the Author

Bhakti Tīrtha Swami was born John E. Favors in a pious, God-fearing family. As a child evangelist, he appeared regularly on television, and as a young man, he was a leader in Dr. Martin Luther King, Jr.'s civil rights movement. At Princeton University, he became president of the student council and also served as chairman of the Third World Coalition. Although his main degree is in psychology, he has received accolades in many other fields, including politics, African studies, and international law.

Bhakti Tīrtha Swami's books are used as reference texts in universities and leadership organizations throughout the world. Many of his books have been printed in English, German, French, Spanish, Portuguese, Macedonian, Croatian, Russian, Hebrew, Slovenian, Balinese, and Italian.

His Holiness has served as assistant coordinator for penal reform programs in the State of New Jersey, Office of the Public Defender, and as a director of several drug abuse clinics in the United States. In addition, he has been a special consultant for Educational Testing Services in the U.S.A. and has managed campaigns for politicians. Bhakti Tīrtha Swami gained international recognition as a representative of the Bhaktivedanta Book Trust, particularly for his outstanding work with scholars in the former communist countries of Eastern Europe.

Bhakti Tīrtha Swami directly oversaw projects in the United States (particularly Washington D.C., Potomac, Maryland, Detroit, Pennsylvania, West Virginia), West Africa, South Africa, Switzerland, France, Croatia, and Bosnia. He also served as the director of the American Federation of Vaiṣṇava Colleges and Schools.

In the United States, Bhakti Tīrtha Swami was the founder and director of the Institute for Applied Spiritual Technology, director of the International Committee for Urban Spiritual Development, and one of the international coordinators of the Seventh Pan African Congress. Reflecting his wide range of interests, he was also a member of the Institute for Noetic Sciences, the Center for Defense Information, the United Nations Association for America, the National Peace Institute Foundation, the World Future Society, and the Global Forum of Spiritual and Parliamentary Leaders.

A specialist in international relations and conflict resolution, Bhakti Tīrtha Swami constantly traveled around the world and had become a spiritual consultant to many high-ranking members of the United Nations, to various celebrities, and to several chiefs, kings, and high court justices. In 1990, His Holiness was coronated as a high chief in Warri, Nigeria in recognition for his outstanding work in Africa and the world. In recent years, he met several times with then-President Nelson Mandela of South Africa to share visions and strategies for world peace.

In addition to encouraging self-sufficiency through the development of schools, clinics, farm projects, and cottage industries, Bhakti Tīrtha Swami conducted seminars and workshops on principle-centered leadership, spiritual development, interpersonal relationships, stress and time management, and other pertinent topics. He was also widely acknowledged as a viable participant in the resolution of global conflict.

On August 5, 2004, Bhakti Tīrtha Swami was diagnosed with melanoma cancer in his left foot. Although he made every effort to treat his condition, the cancer continued to spread, leading His Holiness to teach the most important lesson—how to die. During the time after his diagnosis, he gave numerous lectures on the topic and completed a book of meditations, *The Beggar IV: Die Before Dying*, also dedicated to this same topic. Almost a year later, on June 27, 2005, His Holiness departed from this world, surrounded by loving friends, relatives, and disciples.

Although His Holiness Bhakti Tīrtha Swami has seemingly gone, he actually left behind him a powerful legacy that will continue to live on through his students and well-wishers, and especially through his books. Numerous lectures, seminars, and workshops wait in the archives for Hari-Nama Press to transcribe and to then publish in future books. B.T. Swami's teachings will undoubtedly continue through these unique books and through the lives of those who imbibe his message.

Books and Book Series Available

from Hari-Nama Press by Bhakti Tirtha Swami and others

The Leadership for an Age of Higher Consciousness Series

Leadership in any capacity has taken on such awesome proportions that even the best leaders must find creative ways to deal with today's complex situations. This series includes groundbreaking self-help manuals written for those who seek to develop greater effectiveness in the leadership process.

The Spiritual Warrior Series

The Spiritual Warrior series arms those who answer the call with the spiritual weapons they need to battle debilitating plagues such as depression, anxiety, and hopelessness. B.T. Swami provides us with a series of simple techniques that help us maintain proper perspectives, make better decisions, and achieve uplifting results.

The Beggar Series

Deeply penetrating reflections explore such topics as patience, humility, love, and compassion. The author presents these subjects not as quaint musings from another age but as necessary tools for maintaining sanity in a world of conflict and stress.

The Reflections on Sacred Teachings Series

Through the books in this series, B.T. Swami helps us delve deeper into many of the scriptural teachings of the Vaisnava tradition. In plain, easy to understand language, he allows the reader to apply texts such as Sri Siksastaka and Harinama Cintamani to daily life. In other words, he provides us with ancient wisdom for modern times.

Black Lotus: The Spiritual Journey of an Urban Mystic

This volume explores the life and mission of His Holiness Bhakti Tirtha Swami, an African-American seeker who rose from impoverished beginnings to become a dynamic worldwide spiritual leader. Black Lotus is an uplifting story enriched by the personal testimony of family, friends, college professors, mentors, disciples and fellow travelers on the spiritual path. By Steven Rosen.

Printed in Great Britain
by Amazon

60946870R00104